Pushing Back the Gates

In the series

Philadelphia Voices, Philadelphia Visions
EDITED BY DAVID W. BARTELT

Also in this series:

Ayumi Takenaka and Mary Johnson Osirim, eds., *Global Philadelphia:
Immigrant Communities Old and New*

Carolyn Adams, David Bartelt, David Elesh, and Ira Goldstein, *Restructuring
the Philadelphia Region: Metropolitan Divisions and Inequality*

Richardson Dilworth, ed., *Social Capital in the City: Community and
Civic Life in Philadelphia*

Pushing Back
the Gates

Neighborhood Perspectives on University-Driven
Revitalization in West Philadelphia

Harley F. Etienne

TEMPLE UNIVERSITY PRESS
PHILADELPHIA

TEMPLE UNIVERSITY PRESS
Philadelphia, Pennsylvania 19122
www.temple.edu/tempress

Library of Congress Cataloging-in-Publication Data

Etienne, Harley F., 1974–
    Pushing back the gates : neighborhood perspectives on university-driven
revitalization in West Philadelphia / Harley F. Etienne.
        p. cm. — (Philadelphia voices, Philadelphia visions)
    Includes bibliographical references and index.
    ISBN 978-1-4399-0068-0 (cloth : alk. paper) — ISBN 978-1-4399-0070-3
(e-book)   1. Community development, Urban—Pennsylvania—
Philadelphia.   2. Urban renewal—Pennsylvania—Philadelphia.
3. Community and college—Pennsylvania—Philadelphia.
4. University towns—Pennsylvania—Philadelphia.   5. University of
Pennsylvania.   I. Title.
    HN80.P5E85 2012
    307.1'4160974811—dc23

                                                                    2011051570

ISBN 978-1-4399-0069-7 (paperback : alk. paper)

Printed in the United States of America

090313-P

For Fritz and Anne-Marie and "Cool Whip"

Contents

Preface

Midway through my graduate studies at Temple University in Philadelphia, I read Lisa Redfield Peattie's *Rethinking Ciudad Guyana*, which was a transformative experience. Peattie's illustration of how sociocultural anthropology could be used to assess the impacts of planning made more sense to me than almost anything ever has. Not long after that experience, I came to understand West Philadelphia on a much deeper level. It was fascinating to be a part of the love–hate, multilayered relationship between this diverse, dynamic neighborhood and its institutions. Not long after I arrived in West Philadelphia, a six-alarm blaze took the lives of two of my neighbors and everything I owned. In the wake of the fire and several other high-profile events, the tensions between the University of Pennsylvania and the community were clearer than ever, and I decided then to study the relationship between the two. That master's thesis turned into a dissertation and now this book, and I am still certain that there is more to this complex relationship than I will never know.

While I drafted this manuscript in 2009, a series of news reports started coming out about New York University's plans to expand its campus by 40 percent over the next twenty-five years.[1] The response from residents of New York's East Village was quick, predictable, and consistent with what I found in West Philadelphia and with similar cases across the country. The new "global-networked university" is both placeless and more dependent on place than ever. More and more, universities are aspiring to become global in their reach and nimble in how they produce knowledge, service students, and finance their operations. University leaders walk a high wire every day as they attempt to tend to local and immediate needs both on and off campus while simultaneously aspiring to fulfill grander visions of what their institutions can become.

Many urban residents of medium to large cities in the United States (and perhaps the world) have a relationship of some kind with an institution of higher education. Perspectives on the roles and responsibilities of colleges and universities to their surrounding neighborhoods and larger cities varies widely. With this book, I intend to share the results of a study through which I sought to understand and summarize those perspectives in West Philadelphia. Moreover, I sought to understand whether universities that engage in urban real estate development, urban revitalization, community outreach, service learning, or some combination of those endeavors might use these perspectives to understand what their neighbors think about them and their work, and if they might help schools do things differently or better. With this book, I want to help college and university administrators—squeezed between demands for campuses that are safer and more attractive for high-performing students and faculty and tight budgets and competing agendas—answer that question.

Most important, I speak to West Philadelphia and neighborhoods like it in East Cleveland, Harlem, East Baltimore, South Central Los Angeles, New Haven, Austin, Columbus, and other places that sit adjacent to large institutions whose needs for expansion and development are constant.[2] A critical challenge in the relationship between neighborhoods and large universities is accessible and mutually agreeable goals, direction, and metrics of progress and impacts. As they do in other areas, universities often frame the discourse around the benefits and impacts of their urban engagement and redevelopment work. So then, can colleges and universities that need to expand and are governed by competing factions, offices, and stake-holders "hear" what their neighbors are saying to them?

Planners and policy makers as well may gain something from this work that is not directly tied to debates about community and economic development, affordable housing, or workforce development. It might resemble a classic debate within planning: Which do we care more about—how the decisions were made or the reasons we made them in the first place? Stated differently, do we care if residents were included in the decision making and that their needs were considered? Alternatively, do we care about the political economy of race and class that, for example, positioned the university's self-produced imperative to rehabilitate West Philadelphia above other policy initiatives? In the years since the initiation of the university's revitalization efforts, reliable data on the socioeconomic circumstances of West Philadelphians have been unavailable. When firm quantitative numbers on displacement, changes in income, and other demographics are unavailable, how do we measure impacts of this project?

My project deliberately sought to marshal the perspectives of neighborhood residents and not to challenge the university's own collateral on the topic of university-driven change. The university, neighborhood residents, and interested observers are all handling asymmetrical information. That is, there are details about individual projects and initiatives that are known only to some within the university. Given how complex universities are as institutions, this is a situation impossible to avoid. And, as corporate entities, universities may deliberately withhold full details because they fear the reproach of community groups who mistrust the university no matter what it chooses to do.

This book is an attempt to move the discussion of university-driven development toward the type of rigorous examination that nonuniversity planning efforts undergo. The dynamics of university culture and politics make it bad form to judge one's own institution, but those dynamics are not themselves above examination. How is such work to be included when academics operate in a world where collegial relationships with scholars at other institutions are essential?

In my view, the engagement of colleges and universities (as well as hospitals, museums, and other civic institutions) in large-scale real estate development *is* planning. And as planning, it should be subject to the same assessment and scrutiny that other forms of planning face. Given a scarcity of resources, cities often celebrate any investment or engagement colleges and universities offer. Thus, projects of this type seem to occur beyond the scrutiny and approval processes of municipal planning commissions.

The upgrading of real estate already owned by a university is not a matter for debate and is not covered comprehensively in this book. That said, the focus of these off-grid plans and their external and internal validity are all important areas for academic inquiry. More important, emerging discourses on "anchor institutions" suggest that governments might turn increasingly to their "sticky capital" (immobile generators of economic activity and employment) for momentum in development and revitalization planning.

What this book is not is a compendium of every perspective and detail of Penn's West Philadelphia Initiatives. Former university president Judith Rodin and her colleagues have catalogued and analyzed those efforts well in numerous publications. Those documents largely provide a description of urban revitalization from the perspective of the anchor institution as actor. If details about the university's actions, intentions, or efforts are missing here, such a lack reflects what I learned from those I spoke with. Needless to say, I could have spent the past fifteen years speaking to every West Philadelphia resident, current and former, and I would still not have a full sense of how the area's transformation has helped or changed their lives.

The almost ubiquitous "knee-jerk" reactions to university-driven neighborhood revitalization and change should also be assessed and understood. It is probably unfair and intellectually irresponsible to reduce this phenomenon to a conservative impulse against change.[3] Embedding knee-jerk reactions within the longer histories of town–gown tensions as well as within a larger political economy of class hierarchies, racism, and exclusion that operate in the same places is a formidable task. The residents of a community may not be just blindly reacting negatively to all university-driven proposals but instead speaking more to the powerlessness they feel in contemporary real estate development and planning. In our current age, it may seem that there is no systematic evidence that organized communities can redirect corporate real estate development in directions that are advantageous to them or, at the very least, not detrimental.

I have no qualms about suggesting that city planners are naturally attracted to "workable" solutions to urban problems. If resource-rich institutions such as Penn are interested in urban revitalization for their own "enlightened self-interest," city planners are wise to respond by clearing the hurdles. The challenge for communities is to organize in their own interests, develop their own plans, and work toward their own ideas for neighborhood improvement.

There is still a resource differential that will not allow most low-income communities to replicate what many universities are able to accomplish with even the most modest of investments. The larger challenge is to determine how to repair the social and economic fabric of communities that lack an institution like Penn. Moreover, even if communities do host a university, are the hopes and plans of the two in accord with one another? The assumption of exclusion and asymmetry is unavoidable. And the elite nature of private university education and research in the United States—particularly among a select group of schools in Penn's peer group—makes this is even more the case.

So the photo on the cover of this book becomes a metaphor for the relationship between a large university and its neighbors. Sidewalks can come in various forms. In modern-day America they are often solid concrete, wide, and distinct in form and purpose. Despite the efforts to tame nature and create walkable spaces for people, the vegetation we are trying to control and inhibit finds the cracks and pushes through. In most cases, the construction of sidewalks is an easily achievable goal for planners, civil engineers, and contractors. However, our view of the uses of sidewalks can overlook the various ways people, animals, and even plants may use it in ways different from the ways it was intended to be used. This book attempts to show different perspectives on how a well-intentioned university might fail to see how life will push through its plans.

Acknowledgments

No matter how a writer feels about a project, it must come to an end, and when the end comes, there are people to thank. This work has been on my radar since December 1996 in one form or another. Given that this is my first book (and I hope not my last), my thanks go to all of those who contributed directly to the project and to those who, through their kindness, support, and assistance, aided me in creating the circumstances in which such a project could be pursued.

I benefited from the counsel of several advisors—specifically, Susan M. Christopherson, John Forester, Davydd Greenwood, and Ann-Margaret Esnard—all of whom read drafts undeserving of their attention and yet provided invaluable advice. Before going to Cornell, I benefited from the help of David Bartelt, Michele Masucci, Melissa Gilbert, Judith Goode, and Ricki Sanders. Others who were affiliated with both Temple University Press and Cornell provided critical feedback and advice along the way, including James Earl Davis and Ben Kohl. My time in Philadelphia was enhanced by my connections with professional colleagues and "family," including Craig E. F. Alston, Sam Katz, Ellen Mattleman Kaplan, Claire Marazzo Greenwood, Betty McAdams, Graham Finney, and Cheryl Weiss. They provided me with incredible access to the city's movers, shakers, and decision makers who added to my knowledge of Philadelphia.

I am eternally indebted to Cornell's faculty, staff, and students, whom I learned from, worked for, and received immeasurable assistance from both during and after my time above Cayuga's waters. Specifically, I thank Terry Plater, Keith Hjortshoj, Cornell University's Graduate School, Neema Kudva, Rolf Pendall, Mildred Warner, Ken Reardon, Ariana Vigil, Abdulrazack Karriem, Ella Silverman, Marcel Ionescu-Heroiu, and my brilliant classmates in City and Regional Planning and at Cornell at large. My fraternity brothers in Alpha Phi Alpha, especially Charles Stewart and Kenneth Robinson, deserve mention for keeping me sane in Ithaca.

This book would have been impossible without help from members of the West Philadelphia and University of Pennsylvania communities, many of whom were interviewed and cannot be named here. There are a select few I can name—Ira Harkavy, John Puckett, Vivian Gadsden, Lucy Kerman, Amy Hillier, and the staff at the Cartographic Modeling Laboratory—who were incredibly helpful and supportive of my efforts.

My colleagues and students at Georgia Tech, my current institution, deserve mention here for their support and assistance: Alan Balfour, Jacqueline Royster, Bruce Stiftel, Catherine Ross, Dan Immergluck, Brian Stone, Douglas Allen, Sabir Khan, Mark Cottle, Michael Dobbins, Jennifer Clark, Benjamin Flowers, Cheryl Leggon, Doug Noonan, Gordon Kingsley, the faculties of the Schools of City and Regional Planning and Public Policy, Robin Jernigan, Josh Levin, and my students. I also owe a debt to other planners and professional colleagues: Stacey Sutton, Karen Chapple, Elliott Tretter, Jeffrey Lowe, June Thomas, Elizabeth Sweet, and Lisa Bates.

My largest debt is to my close friends and family for their unwavering support: Linda Etienne, Judy Polyne, Antonine Polyne, Joseph Hughes, Chantale Nicholas-Deetjean, Yves Deetjean, Darrell Tiller, and Tony L. Burks II. I owe a special thanks to Alita Anderson and the larger Anderson/Golden clan, Chantal Laroche-Veira, Manu Platt, and David Malebranche for encouragement and invaluable support.

I also thank some unmentionable friends and others who contributed to this project in various ways. I am especially grateful to my
parents, Fritz and Anne-Marie Etienne, who taught me the lesson of
displacement and bestowed on me an intense interest in cities and in
university–community relations in particular. My brother and friend
Millery Polyne deserves many thanks for understanding the struggle
of academic writing and having my back since 1974.

Last and most important, I am incredibly thankful for the study's
participants; I cannot name them, but they are worthy of my eternal
gratitude. Any errors or omissions here are mine alone and not those
of anyone mentioned here or the countless people I did not name
who provided assistance.

Pushing Back the Gates

I

Cities and Their Universities

Logical Places to Search for Hope

In the wake of the "Great Recession," there are many questions about how the U.S. economy will ultimately rebound and which institutions will help make recovery happen. The losses to the manufacturing, banking, and housing sectors have been nothing short of sensational. A common mantra spoken by politicians and pundits is that innovation will lead recovery and re-create the American economy in the coming years and decades. To a great extent, this is true. And investments in human capital and in the technological advancements that will increase future American competitiveness will most likely come out of American colleges and universities—particularly American research universities.

Yet many do not understand how universities work or how important they are to their local contexts or to the nation at large. The socially accepted narrative about universities is that they are wealthy, geographically bound islands of privilege and exclusivity with significant resources. In this narrative, colleges and universities are largely benign, and their impacts on society are generally beneficent and magnanimous, taking the form of education for society or breakthroughs in research; thus, universities are responsible for proving their own usefulness to society. In the face of declining public sector support for community revitalization, this narrative expands to include an obligation to resolve urban social problems and generate economic development at both local and regional levels. If Herbert Rubin is correct that economic developers must "shoot anything that flies; claim anything that falls," then universities—particularly research universities—become just one of those things.[1] Cities and their economic development professionals cannot make colleges and universities contribute to local economic development. They can only hope that the universities will. They are a form of "sticky capital," which means that they are fixed in place and unable to operate completely in virtual worlds or offshore, as other corporate entities so often choose to do.

This chapter provides some historical background for these assumptions and discusses why many universities affirm the narratives about them. I contend that many colleges and universities, particularly those that are research oriented, are complex institutions that must serve many purposes. Teaching is but one of the roles they play, but it is often the aspect of academic life that receives the most attention from those who cannot see the intense focus on research happening within universities. Research and knowledge production have grown to dwarf other activities as the race to commercialize research and expand its economic benefits to institutions and their host cities and regions accelerates. Budget reductions in the most recent era have placed even more emphasis on sponsored research and the need to create new spaces for it. After decades of decline, many cities and metropolitan areas are now, at the beginning of the new millennium, starting to enjoy dynamic and dramatic reversals of fortune, which were nearly erased by the economic downtown that began in 2008.[2] The dynamics of evolving postindustrial landscapes in northern and northeastern American cities reflect new modes of planning and policy making for urban regeneration. The new focus on improvements in quality of life instead of alleviation of poverty has brought new stakeholders to the forefront of urban revitalization. Among these new stakeholders are colleges and universities, whose role in the revitalization of urban places and neighborhoods is ever increasing.[3]

This book presents findings from a study of a neighborhood revitalization project in which a private research university became a significant driver of change. At the center of the University City section of West Philadelphia sits the University of Pennsylvania (Penn),[4] which between 1994 and 2004 implemented a comprehensive project that is now regarded as one of the most important examples of university-driven urban revitalization.[5] At the start of the 1990s, Penn found itself surrounded by crime, dilapidated housing, poorly performing schools, and poverty, and confronted with a lack of amenities to serve its students, staff, and faculty.[6] To address the concerns of students, their parents, alumni, and other constituents, the university developed a systematic plan of action for dealing with conditions in West Philadelphia.

The central questions of this book are these: (1) How have the neighborhoods of University City and West Philadelphia changed since the inception of the West Philadelphia Initiatives? (2) How has the university's revitalization effort contributed to those changes? (3) How have the university-driven changes benefited University City's various neighborhoods and constituencies? (4) To what extent did other, competing revitalization efforts and/or social trends contribute to the success of the university's efforts and the distribution of its subsequent benefits? These questions are answered through neighborhood-level perspectives of change in the ethnographic accounts given here. This study provides a more balanced view of the role universities play in urban revitalization—something that quantitative demographic and housing data cannot offer.

While this study reviews many of the university's activities, it is not a comprehensive evaluation of them. Instead, it seeks to contribute to broader academic and policy discourses on urban neighborhood change and the role that interested universities are now playing in their host communities and urban places. This is a narrative of the impacts that neighborhood change—university driven and other— has had on the lives of University City/West Philadelphia residents; it is not an assessment of the university's efforts. Nor is it a canonical text against which other narratives of Penn's impacts on West Philadelphia should be assessed. The narratives and perspectives here should be balanced against other information and placed in their proper context. However, the perceptions of West Philadelphia residents are instructive exactly as they are and without defensive posturing and finger wagging from the university's administration. It is important that the residents' assessments of the process and their perspectives on it stand as credible information—even if they may be misinformed or factually wrong from the perspectives of others.

This book and its conclusions present evidence from the West Philadelphia/University of Pennsylvania case that explains how Penn responded to the challenges of its location in an economically marginal section of the city. It also presents evidence of how the university's efforts were, in many ways, aided and occasionally impeded by various competing efforts and broader economic and social trends. What follows is an introduction to the wider significance of this topic and to the case study that is the core of this book.

The rationale for my methodological approach was to test the hypothesis that the University of Pennsylvania's urban revitalization efforts were the primary source of neighborhood change and improvement in the University City area of West Philadelphia. My research shows that this hypothesis did not consider that an array of nonuniversity-related factors also contributed to neighborhood change.

The book is based primarily on an ethnographic study that examined resident impressions of neighborhood change. The interviews were mostly with current and former residents of the University City and West Philadelphia neighborhoods closest to the Penn campus, and with Penn staff and students. The project had multiple perspectives because the informants directed the research through their referrals of additional informants and their suggestions of new questions for those subsequent interviews. For example, informants were responsible for helping to shift the original focus away from the university's efforts to nonuniversity-driven policies, trends, and revitalization programs as agents of neighborhood change. However, qualitative accounts data show a more nuanced and complex picture where gains in many areas created difficulties in others. In the absence of longitudinal demographic and housing data, ethnographic narratives of neighborhood change showed themselves to be an effective way to gauge the true impacts of the university's efforts.

In all, forty-two structured and unstructured interviews occurred between November 2004 and July 2006. The ethnographic portion of the study was a variation of Heckathorn's respondent-driven sampling method or, more accurately, a network ethnography.[7] The theoretical and methodological approach presumed that accounts of informants would demonstrate that change had occurred while not providing sufficient evidence of a causal relationship between the university initiatives and the informants' own perceptions.

Unlike other studies of university–community engagement, this book does not assume that resourceful elite institutions like Penn should or can serve as buoys for troubled inner-city communities; nor does it assume that such institutions should or can avoid the sometimes harsh realities of those places. While I hope that my research informs other urban colleges and universities and the communities that border them, some of what I present here is not entirely generalizable. Indeed, I took care to treat the West Philadelphia/University of Pennsylvania case as unique. The history of University City, Penn, and this "model" revitalization program is an informative narrative that comprises a particular mix of university initiative, an evolving social world in West Philadelphia's neighborhoods, and changes in urban redevelopment paradigms and policy. I demonstrate that notions of success are in many ways yet to be determined and far more complex than the quantitative and spatial analysis of neighborhood change can currently show. While the interviews and qualitative data focused on the period of the university's most intense engagement, informants provided information, spanning as much as eighty years, on the history and evolution of various West Philadelphia neighborhoods, their lives, and their views of the university.

In recent years, optimism about the role that higher education plays in urban development has grown.[8] As the subsequent chapters discuss, this hopefulness is situated in the current historical moment, when universities (and their advocates) have come to recognize the university's potential to act as a buoy of metropolitan economies and local housing markets. The current state of our global and national economies and local housing markets has only heightened this reality. In turn, local context is important for universities that find themselves competing for talented students, staff, and faculty, and in need of marketplaces for the commercialization of university-generated research. To that end, the knowledge economy, and the universities that drive it, have the potential to reorganize urban space to serve their interests, as industrial capital did in the nineteenth and twentieth centuries.

Simultaneously, the evolving social and economic landscape of the American city has become increasingly prominent in the academic literature of planning, urban sociology, anthropology, and geography. As used here, the term *neighborhood change* captures the diversity of the literature on the subject. A central interest of this study is the more specific and hard-to-define term *urban revitalization*, which, at its most basic, implies improvement or upgrading and can encompass physical, economic, and social aspects of urban places.[9] *Revitalization* has come to imply and represent a particular form of urban renaissance. However, consensus on its definition and approaches to it remain elusive. Like many planning terms, it is political in that it generates more debates than it settles.[10]

In discussing the contrast between downtown and neighborhood redevelopment and the focus on aesthetic and physical improvements, urban sociologist David Bartelt poses this question: For whom are we saving the cities?[11] As to this study of Penn's work in West Philadelphia, the question might be recast: For whom did Penn save West Philadelphia?

I argue throughout the book that a definition of revitalization that considers metrics of social disparities and incumbent upgrading is no longer a prominent one in the literature of planning and social science.[12] While many neoliberal commentators have declared victory for *place-based* and *market-based* redevelopment, others question the ability of these approaches to engage the structural causes of urban decline and poverty such as racial discrimination and global/metropolitan economic restructuring.[13] Advocates of place-based and market-based redevelopment appear willing to bypass this debate in the interest of expedient and achievable results in urban upgrading;

however, critics have predicted and cited cases where these redevelopment approaches are not beneficial to marginalized and disadvantaged populations.[14] This conflict may be a result of a neoliberal turn in urban and antipoverty policy that began during the 1980s and 1990s.

A different but relevant issue is that of displacement. Redevelopment plans and trends that fail to address poverty often create episodes of poverty through the direct physical displacement of the poor to make way for new residential development. This can also happen indirectly through decreases in affordable housing that occur when neighborhoods are valorized. The default negative assessment of displacement caused by such redevelopment has been dismissed by some as anti-intellectual sentimentality, a conservative impulse, a fear of commerce and development, and a fear of change.[15] This view may also reflect a weariness of catering to the special interests of minority communities by presuming that any change victimizes them.

Recent scholarship on gentrification has gone even further, suggesting that disadvantaged populations are often not only agents of significant neighborhood change or gentrification but their beneficiaries as well.[16] This book presents evidence that many West Philadelphia residents resisted how West Philadelphia was changing but simultaneously benefited from the changes. Although, through its work in West Philadelphia, Penn contributed to improvements in public safety, public education, local housing, and retail amenities, various University City neighborhoods and constituent groups have not evenly enjoyed the benefits of West Philadelphia's revival.

The data and findings presented here challenge current literature on university-driven neighborhood revitalization, in large part because they are critical of the university's potential to influence and direct urban revitalization since such work distracts from its central mission. At the same time, this book seeks to fill a void in the literature on universities and cities. Much of the current writing falls into one of two categories. The first is applause for the good that universities promise and often achieve for urban neighborhoods. The second is a visceral attack on the "failure" of universities to meet their implicit obligations to the public interest.[17] In many ways case studies of university engagement may best be catalogued and analyzed by those with primary access to the narratives of institutional decision making; however, these writings risk being interpreted as skewed because of their authors' loyalty to larger institutional interests. In this case study I strive to analyze the work colleges and universities perform in cities in a critical and balanced way.

A critical study of a large institution risks demonizing that institution. Given the long and tumultuous history of "town–gown" relations in the United States, it is tempting to prejudge and distrust all plans for university-led urban redevelopment. Penn's town-gown history has been particularly troubled. Land acquisitions for dramatic campus expansions made during the late 1960s and early 1970s displaced thousands of poor and working poor families, many of them African American.[18] As Margaret Pugh O'Mara's *Cities of Knowledge* demonstrates, the relationship of universities to cities—and neighborhood revitalization projects in particular—is best approached from a perspective that encompasses local and national events. In the contemporary era, an understanding of university-based plans for neighborhood revitalization should be connected to multiple scales of analysis and broader trends.

This study is based on a political-economic perspective of urban development and policy. As a social phenomenon, I understand urban problems in the United States to be inextricably tied to the history of racial discrimination in labor and housing markets. Those problems are also intimately tied to the economic reorganization of cities based on new modes of production; federal, state, and local government policy; and the phenomenon of poverty that is related to all of these factors. This perspective conflicts with the emerging idea that impoverished neighborhoods can (and perhaps should) be revitalized without taking into consideration the pernicious effects of racism on local housing markets.[19]

In the planning and development paradigm, where real estate development serves as a proxy for community development, neighborhood revitalization schemes are not obliged to address the structural sources of poverty and social dislocation. My perspective is that the short-term success of urban real estate development masks the persistent problem of urban poverty that was unresolved by the New Deal policies of the 1950s and 1960s and in fact was exacerbated by restructured urban economies and neoliberal public policy of the 1980s and 1990s. The fragmentation of municipal governance and services created openings for private actors to complete what public policy failed to do—make inner city neighborhoods attractive and livable.[20] The shift of responsibility from the federal government to cash-strapped city governments created opportunities for colleges and universities to augment municipal services such as crime prevention.[21] For better or worse, this placed the fate of urban communities in the hands of private actors who are not directly accountable to public processes or interests.

Another important part of this narrative is an understanding of how higher education operates and has evolved over time. The relationship between cities and their institutions of higher education goes back to medieval times.[22] In the United States, this relationship has evolved against a backdrop of rising industrial production; several waves of migrants from Europe, the American South, the Caribbean, Asia, and South America; deindustrialization; and the urban crisis that followed.[23] As a way of responding to critics of higher education, many institutional leaders have suggested that universities should deepen their ties to their host communities.[24] Those ties have taken various forms, including partner and catalyst for economic growth, collaborator in urban neighborhood revitalization projects, and provider of urban services.[25]

"Eds" and "meds"—colleges/universities and hospitals—are often cited as potential factors in the revival of urban economies and communities.[26] In the past two decades, higher education and health care became two of the largest sources of employment in contemporary urban economies. Fleeing capital has played an important role in creating hubs of higher education and healthcare (which are often joined), leading to islands of growth and wealth in many economically stagnant and declining urban areas.[27] We can define universities in many ways but most easily by their geographic location(s) and by their "product"—that is, their students, who will become central actors in the knowledge economy. The shift from Taylorist forms of production to science- and technology-driven development has made higher education and specifically research universities more important than ever.

Society expects a great deal from universities, as universities expect a great deal from themselves. Local, state, and federal support in the form of direct subsidies and tax-exempt status makes them implicitly accountable to the world beyond their campuses, although this has not always been the dominant perspective. In exchange for subsidies, universities are expected to advance the interests of society through their knowledge production and, more recently, through their service provision (payments in lieu of taxes [PILOTS]), hiring, and local spending.[28] Like corporations, colleges, universities, and hospitals often employ hundreds and sometimes thousands of workers, many of whom have college or advanced degrees. Colleges and universities are embracing the philosophy of engagement to respond to pressure that they become more engaged. That pressure, however, is now balanced with the discovery of how urban spaces are important to universities as context for their institutions and as marketplaces for their products, research, and graduates.

This book also seeks to inform urban communities that anchor college or university campuses. For them, physical proximity to a campus represents many opportunities, but it also holds risks. In addition to being providers of employment, education and training, and even rental income, campuses are emerging as major destinations for retail shopping, cultural and sporting events, and amenities. The risk for communities hosting these campuses comes in various forms but most often in competition for land, customers, tenants, and the like. When universities seek to expand their campuses where space is scarce, they must assemble parcels through land acquisition.

Communities interested in their own redevelopment are keen to understand how private organizations leverage their activities to support their own efforts and interests. I present evidence from the Penn case that suggests where the risks and opportunities of community-university collaboration may lie. The pressures that compel universities to compete for top students and faculty may influence their agendas and vision as well as their contributions to neighborhood renewal in ways that run counter to community-based revitalization objectives. Issues involving decreasing housing affordability, diversity, and social cohesion are created and/or exacerbated if the revitalization agendas of a university and its community are not compatible.

Naturally, this book also seeks to inform academic and practicing planners interested in inner-city renewal and neighborhood revitalization. In responding to calls for public accountability, planners and developers measure growth and renewal in fairly narrow and econometric terms. However, the question must be asked: Are the social costs of a particular development pattern less important than the economic gains? The issue is recognized—an increase in poor households paying a greater proportion of their incomes on rent and a decrease in housing options represent a problem of great interest to planners and economists.[29] Given the history and political economy of race and class in U.S. cities, it stands to reason that we must understand for whom urban places are rehabilitated and by what methods. Yet planning thought and much social science literature have drifted away from these concerns, as have government interest and commitment. Although it might seem ridiculous to suggest that planners are antiurban, it is arguable that the planning field has turned away from poverty and race in favor of profit-seeking or profit-maximizing physical planning and real estate development.[30] The decline of topics such as equity and advocacy planning speaks to this shift in the planning literature. By "problematizing" the University of Pennsylvania's definition of revitalization, I hope to contribute to a larger debate about how planners, communities, and others concerned about cities gauge the extent and impacts of inner-city revitalization and change.

The changes that affect inner-city neighborhoods as a result of university-driven development have significant implications for the racial and social integration of urban and suburban places. I contend that a significant part of Penn's interest in neighborhood revitalization and change is its need for its real estate investments to succeed. Success is focused not on profit but on creating amenities to satisfy the discriminating tastes of top students and faculty.[31]

The conclusions of this study suggest that, unlike industrial capitalism, the knowledge economy may create a privileged and exclusive territory on top of an existing social hierarchy. While race and class are still significant factors in determining access to resources, university-led development contributes to another layer of exclusion in the evolving urban landscape.[32] The spatial reorganization of urban space by a university in the name of revitalization symbolizes the knowledge economy's marginalization of the poor and already disenfranchised. For inner-city residents, this may affect their access to resources and social networks at various levels.[33] I treat the fortunes of low-income communities in this new context as a way of more broadly analyzing how these groups are (again) separated from the locus of well-paying jobs, investment, and dynamic economic activity in metropolitan regions.

2

West Philadelphia, the University of Pennsylvania, and the Rough Road to Revival and Cooperation

For many reasons, the West Philadelphia/University of Pennsylvania case is one of the most notable examples of university-driven revitalization and university–community collaboration. In the mid-1960s, Penn began to develop strategies for improving campus life. This required expansion into previously residential and commercial strips, which led to a continuing need for negotiating a new relationship with surrounding communities. To that end, in the 1990s Penn developed both an infrastructure for community engagement and service learning and a parallel and somewhat complementary real estate development agenda. Together, these systems created one of the most celebrated examples of university-driven urban change and redevelopment. This chapter reviews the history of the university's efforts of the 1990s and early 2000s in order to place them in their proper context.

On Halloween Night in 1996, a purse snatcher fatally stabbed a University of Pennsylvania researcher, Vladimir Sled, on a West Philadelphia sidewalk.[1] In the weeks before Sled's murder, the university had been victimized by a rash of crimes, including the shooting of a student near campus.[2] Although crime was nothing new to West Philadelphia by 1996, Sled's stabbing, in plain view of his girlfriend and twelve-year-old son, struck a painful chord with many West Philadelphia residents and Penn students, faculty, and staff. It exposed long-standing tensions and anxieties about the urban crime that many West Philadelphians had come to accept as their way of life.

At a meeting with concerned parents during the university's homecoming weekend a few weeks later, then Penn president Judith Rodin and then Philadelphia mayor Edward G. Rendell were booed off the stage as they tried to assuage the crowd's fears about crime in the area. Long before this meeting, Rodin and Rendell had known of West Philadelphia's problems and were developing a plan to improve public safety in the area. Nevertheless, they were given their marching orders to clean up the crime or lose students.

Several university staff and administrators interviewed for this study recalled how important that experience was for Rodin and the university. More than any other event, the stabbing served as a major turning point in Penn's resolve to seek solutions to the "West Philadelphia problem." A few days after the parent meeting, a group of area residents held a candlelight vigil in nearby Clark Park to commemorate the life of the slain researcher and to draw attention to the problem of neighborhood crime. The parent meeting and the vigil sparked the emergence of a new wave of activity collectively known now as the West Philadelphia Initiatives (WPI).

As a program for neighborhood revitalization, the WPI were not intended to be a comprehensive plan for the area. Their focus was on five main areas of activity: the fortification of public education, increased housing availability and quality, clean and safe streets, improved economic opportunity for residents, and increased and improved retail options.

According to study participants and other commentators on the Penn/West Philadelphia case, many of the improvements in University City and West Philadelphia were, in some manner, because of the university's efforts. What follows is a history of both Penn and its university–community relations. Placing the WPI in a longer trajectory of tensions and relations between university and community reveals how activity since 1996 represents the apex of work begun by

Penn president Gaylord Harnwell in the 1950s and how that work has been touched by every president of the university since.

Perhaps more than that of any other urban university, the work of the University of Pennsylvania has been well documented at both a local and a national level. However, much of this documentation has been initiated by the university itself.[3] Many in the Penn community would regard Rodin's tenure as president as one of the most successful and distinguished because of her leadership of the WPI and the growth of the institution's prestige and standing.[4] Additionally, Penn's Netter Center for Community Partnerships is internationally known as a model of university–urban engagement and service-learning curricula. To date, much of the writing about Penn's urban engagement and revitalization efforts has been by those closest to the work itself, with other accounts by admirers.

This chapter describes components of the West Philadelphia Initiatives, the greatest impacts of which, according to informants, have been improved conditions in University City and West Philadelphia. There is agreement on a certain amount of improvement, but informants were mixed on the methods, the types of improvements, and the impacts those improvements have had on their lives. The final section of this chapter presents informants' views of the university and the West Philadelphia Initiatives.

An Abbreviated "Urban" History of the University of Pennsylvania

The University of Pennsylvania holds a special place in the history of American higher education. Chartered in 1749 by Benjamin Franklin, it was the brainchild of Franklin along with civic, social, and commercial leaders who felt that Philadelphia needed a university in order to join the ranks of other world-class cities.[5] In the mid-eighteenth century, Franklin authored a treatise on the need to train the territory's youth for practical arts. His famous essay, "A Proposal for the Education of the Youth of Pennsylvania [sic]" laid the groundwork not just for the University of Pennsylvania but for secular higher education in the United States.[6] Franklin's essay led to the founding of an academy that would later become the University of Pennsylvania in 1791. Unlike its colonial peers, Franklin's academy would focus on preparing men not for the clergy but for commerce and public service. Today, Penn's programs in business, medicine, nursing, dentistry, and law are considered some of the best in the nation and are among the oldest. While debate continues as to which U.S. college first made the move to a research orientation, Penn often claims this honor because of the age and prestige of its various professional schools. For most of its history, however, it remained a teaching college, graduating fewer than five hundred students in 1920.

Despite its long history, Penn has not always been regarded as a true rival to schools such as Harvard and Yale. Its admittance into the Ivy League athletic conference was a topic of great debate among the other universities in the league, based on its reputation as a "football school with lacking academics."[7] Penn differed from many universities in that its various parts, until very recently, operated virtually autonomously, with only a loose affiliation to the larger institution. Moreover, its administration lacked structure and recognizable leadership. Penn did not have a university president until the inauguration of Thomas Sovereign Gates in 1930.[8] Until then, for the most part, the board of trustees governed the affairs of the university and arguably failed to control the units that sought to assert their independence when necessary.[9] John Terino describes the process by which the University of Pennsylvania pursued the status of research powerhouse equivalent to that of its respected peers and thereby became a greater beneficiary of the federal government's Cold War spending on science and technology.[10] Its disorganized and divided engineering and science schools were in need not only of facilities and faculty but also of direction and mission. Finally, the institution found both with President Gaylord Harnwell, who led the university between 1953 and 1970. Under his leadership, Penn began working with city groups and leaders to construct the University City Science Center, an independent center of innovation that would provide Philadelphia and the universities located in West Philadelphia with a foothold in the new military-industrial complex. Harnwell is also credited with diversifying the university and dramatically expanding its size, constructing ninety-three buildings during his tenure.

In the late nineteenth century, confronted with Philadelphia's dominance as an industrial power, Penn made the transition from a teaching college to a Humboldtian-model research institution. This identity was not an enormous leap given Penn's mission for and orientation toward its already prestigious professional schools. Throughout most of the nineteenth century, Penn was known as the "University of the State of Pennsylvania." Because it was regarded in the eighteenth century as a haven for Tory sympathizers, it was renamed and rechartered by the city fathers as a state affiliate, further indebting its graduates and faculty toward a mission that favored the city and the state.[11]

Since its founding, the University of Pennsylvania has operated at three distinct sites. The first location was at Fourth and Chestnut Streets, in what is now known as "Society Hill" and is the oldest part of the city. Franklin himself worked, lived, and was buried a few short blocks away. The university moved to its second location at Ninth and Chestnut in 1901.[12] Finding itself again surrounded by teeming urban life, the university moved for a third and last time to the Almshouse Farm on the western banks of the Schuylkill River, then suburban farmland. This move represented a major shift in university life. Penn was now somewhat divorced from the ills of the city, although in a few short decades, the city would come to surround the West Philadelphia campus as it had in central Philadelphia.

Until 1930, Penn's board of trustees was the primary decision-making body of the university, with the deans of the respective colleges and the provost acting as day-to-day managers and chiefs of their respective units. Because it was not until the 1940s that Penn had a strong senior administration, its academic structure did not become fully integrated until Judith Rodin's tenure in the late 1990s.

Although Penn's professional schools flourished during the nineteenth and early twentieth centuries, its undergraduate curriculum proved disconnected at best. For the better part of its history, Penn's academic reputation was largely regional. As previously mentioned, its admission into the Ivy League was highly contested by the already admitted universities, whose argument was that Penn was more an athletic than an academic school. After agreeing to dismantle its nationally renowned athletic programs, Penn was admitted to the league.

As Philadelphia continued its industrialization into the twentieth century, a growing population of African Americans from the American South found their way into West Philadelphia. The deindustrialization that followed World War II set the city on a path toward population loss and urban poverty for the next sixty years. During that time, urban blight and decline found its way to the gates of the Penn campus. Immigration forever transformed the character of West Philadelphia's neighborhoods, which changed so fast and so dramatically that a plan, never carried out, was developed by the university trustees to relocate the campus to university-owned property in Valley Forge, Pennsylvania. At virtually the same time, Penn saw itself develop into a true research university comparable to some of the nation's most elite and wealthy institutions. The philanthropy of the city's Protestant industrial elite proved to be one of its best assets as it sought to compete in a marketplace for university research.

Immediately following the decision to remain in West Philadelphia (rather than move to Valley Forge), the end of World War II, and the onset of the Cold War, a race began among the nation's elite research universities to garner a significant share of the federal government's largesse.[13] Largely, Penn succeeded in leveraging its medical school and strengths in information technology and life sciences to spawn the University City Science Center and what has become the Hospital of the University of Pennsylvania complex—consistently one of the nation's leading receivers of funding from the National Institutes of Health (NIH).

A Brief History of University–Community Relations in West Philadelphia

The University of Pennsylvania's history is laced with tensions between its continual attempt to personify a romantic ideal of classical university education and the harsh realities of its industrial and later postindustrial surroundings. This history is marked with a few moments of increased tension between Penn and certain demographic groups based on the notorious displacement of hundreds of African Americans during the period of Urban Renewal in the 1950s and 1960s and several high-profile incidents involving Penn students, faculty, and staff. In the establishment of the University City Science Center, approximately six hundred low-income and African American families were displaced. Unlike other institutions that used the Section 112 amendment of the Urban Renewal legislation of 1949 (which allowed colleges and universities to employ Urban Renewal policy for campus expansion), Penn leveraged that legislation to construct the nation's first inner-city urban research park. The legacy of this event is still experienced by many West Philadelphia residents. Two former residents of "Black Bottom," the area razed in the construction of the center, were interviewed for this study.

Many universities faced with similar challenges have taken different approaches. In her introduction to John Kromer and Lucy Kerman's report on the West Philadelphia Initiatives, former Penn president Judith Rodin outlined Penn's choices in the wake of the new urban crisis in West Philadelphia during the 1990s. Those choices included (1) engaging in community-oriented academic and service-oriented activities, (2) physically sequestering the campus with walls and gates, (3) relocating the campus, and (4) leveraging the university's resources to improve area conditions. These choices represented a higher-education version of Albert Hirschman's theory of exit, voice, and loyalty, where the first choice represents voice, the second and third represent exit, and the fourth represents loyalty.[14]

For many years, the best lens through which to view the university's contentious relations with West Philadelphia was Penn students. Through their often uncivic behavior, students revealed a naiveté regarding urban living and a contempt for and fear of their neighbors. For many years, they received maps of West Philadelphia as a part of their orientation. Those maps contained a black line that explicitly warned students not to travel beyond Fortieth Street (going west) because crime was much higher on the other side. This rationale was a subtext for the reality that the areas west of Fortieth Street were predominately African American. As one participant in this study mentioned, one of the supermarkets located three blocks from the Penn campus, an Acme store, was nicknamed by Penn students "Black-Me" and avoided by students because of its clientele and overall quality.

Some West Philadelphia residents feel that because of Penn's development of high-end retail amenities on and near its campus in the past fifteen years, retail amenities for residents of more limited means have diminished. One of the only remaining retail outlets near the campus that is still patronized by more African Americans than Penn students is a McDonald's directly across the street from the Penn-developed supermarket and movie theater/bistro/nightclub on Fortieth Street. In 2008, the university completed a mixed-use development near this intersection, replacing an aging strip mall with the Radian, a 14-story building with 179 market-rate apartments and 40,000 square feet of retail.[15] Original plans for this development called for the relocation of a long-standing McDonald's restaurant at the corner of Fortieth and Walnut. Attempts to relocate the restaurant to nearby Market Street inspired the Neighbors against McPenntrification group to file a suit to halt the construction of the new building. The group succeeded, and the McDonald's remains in its original location. University representatives have stated that they still wish to help the restaurant to relocate and deny the implication that there are racist or nefarious intentions behind their assistance. In the university's view, the intersection has changed dramatically, and at least in an architectural sense, a one-story, detached, fast food restaurant is no longer needed and does not maximize the utility of its current site. This was understood as the university's blatant and overt racism toward the community. While students no longer receive maps as a part of orientation, the suggestion that West Philadelphia should be transformed to better service Penn students and faculty remains the dominant theme of the area's revitalization efforts.[16]

Over the last forty years, Penn's presidents devoted a great deal of attention to the issue of West Philadelphia. Informants with any opinion on this longer history all agree that the trend has been toward a gradual improvement in the university's position on, and commitment to being an integral part of, West Philadelphia's life and economy. Each president since Gaylord Harnwell, who oversaw the university's expansion under Urban Renewal, spent some part of his or her tenure engaging the question and problem of West Philadelphia.

The university's stance on neighborhood change in West Philadelphia can at best be summarized as driven mostly by self-interest. That interest revolved around the desire to create a "connected and walkable" academic village embedded in an urban community.[17] So far in the twenty-first century, the inter-institutional competition for top faculty, students, research funding and support, and alumni donations has led the University of Pennsylvania to reinvent itself through transformation of its campus and surrounding environs. The impetus for much of this activity began with a focus on on-campus public safety and increased neighborhood desirability. As later chapters discuss, many factions within the university were very interested in social justice and beneficial outreach. However, it is the "emergency" of enhancing the university's context that has dominated its efforts in the most recent era and perhaps well before.

In the words of a Penn administrator, the intention was to "stabilize the area for private investment." The framework for the university's efforts came directly from Ira Harkavy's research and community engagement and directives from the Netter Center for Community Partnerships, which has existed in some form since the 1980s. According to historical records, the university's commitment to West Philadelphia crystallized after proposals to relocate the university campus to its bucolic Valley Forge holdings failed in the 1940s.

In significant ways, the West Philadelphia Initiatives were organized to respond to calls by parents and students for a safer urban environment for this prestigious university community. One of the critics of the WPI offered the following:

> It's as if we now have students who are the children of the scared suburbanites who think they can come to school here and be as safe at three in the morning as they are in the afternoon. This is not [a] completely enclosed community where they are free to do what they want.

Note that Penn is not the only institution of higher education in West Philadelphia. To its north sits Drexel University, previously the Drexel Institute of Technology, an institution that has grown in size and stature since its beginnings over one hundred and twenty years ago. Because of its relatively smaller endowment, Drexel has had its own issues with community tensions, but it has consistently refused and failed to respond in any meaningful way. To the west of Penn's campus sits the Restaurant School, now known as the Restaurant School at Walnut Hill College. And to the south sits the University of the Sciences of Philadelphia (USP), which was formerly known as the Philadelphia College for Pharmaceutical Sciences. Penn students receive the brunt of the criticism for West Philadelphia's town-gown tensions in large part because of their numbers and the extent to which West Philadelphia revolves around Penn's nearly 300 acres.[18]

Besides in physical size, these other schools are smaller than the juggernaut Penn in their employment bases and endowments, which collectively represent only a fraction of Penn's total. Despite this, the physical expansion of the University of Pennsylvania following World War II would provide the context for the often contentious relationship between the university and the West Philadelphia neighborhoods that surround its campus. At several points in that relationship, the university attempted to inspire neighborhood change and revitalization, or leveraged its political and economic influence to see that change happened. Those changes sometimes inspired mutually beneficial transformations but often did not.

The successes of the university's effort have been heralded by its own public relations infrastructure and a series of scholarly works citing the turnaround of West Philadelphia. These successes were not the first for the university; nor were they the beginning of the process. Every Penn president since the end of World War II in some way dealt with the challenges of administrating a major research university in a struggling inner city. The momentum was increased by succeeding presidents, culminating in the 2004 creation of the Penn Compact, a new institutional philosophy that extends Penn's mantra of engagement well beyond West Philadelphia.[19]

Penn's founding in what is now known as "Olde City Philadelphia" cast a mold for its relationship with its urban home that has
always been somewhat uneasy. Like some of its Ivy League counterparts, Penn moved twice since its founding,[20] the rationale for
each move that of placing the university in "an appropriate academic
context." In 1887, nine years prior to Columbia's move from midtown Manhattan to its current home in Morningside Heights, Penn
moved from Center City Philadelphia to its current home in West
Philadelphia, which at that time was primarily farmland and sparsely
populated by summer residents from the city's elite. However, the
construction of several bridges linking Philadelphia's center to West
Philadelphia created a boom in building across the Schuylkill River.
Within fifty years, West Philadelphia closely resembled the bustling
city the university had moved to avoid.

The years between 1930 and 1990 represented a time when
the university attempted to fortify itself against the effects of deindustrialization and the movement of many poor and working-class
families into West Philadelphia communities. The integration and
subsequent racial tipping of several of those communities into predominantly African American neighborhoods furthered the university's resolve to redevelop its environs.

The Emergence of a New Paradigm
of Community Engagement

In their summary of the scope and success of the West Philadelphia
Initiatives, John Kromer and Lucy Kerman provide details of the
university's planning and administration of the WPI and intended
and measured outcomes. This section summarizes interviews with
various university administrators and staff who were involved in the
revitalization effort and provides context that Kromer and Kerman's
report does not.

The University of Pennsylvania's changing stance toward its role
in the urban revitalization of West Philadelphia can best be understood
through the evolution of its philosophy of university–community relations. According to some commentators, Penn is one of the most

exciting universities in the country because of its civic engagement and university-led urban revitalization. The university's "success" has generated a particular self-perspective in the area of university-community relations, which has also developed from the other successes the institution has enjoyed in part because of its university-community work. The inauguration of Amy Gutmann as Penn's eighth president in 2004 led many to hope that Gutmann would continue the work of her predecessors in West Philadelphia. That hope was based on Gutmann's own intellectual biography, and preliminary statements about her plans for the university indicated that she intended to make the university's connections to its local and global contexts cornerstones of her presidency.[21] Her presidency has built not only on the legacy of Judith Rodin, Penn's first alumna president, but also on that of the three Penn presidents—Sheldon Hackney, Martin Meyerson, and Gaylord Harnwell—who preceded Rodin. Since the Harnwell presidency, the University of Pennsylvania has seen the city of Philadelphia, its industry, population, and tax base crumble. The neighborhoods immediately adjacent to the West Philadelphia campus have been, and to some extent remain, among the most distressed in the city. The consequences of this distress have been many, both for the university and for its local context. Penn's geographic proximity to this decline has been perhaps its greatest motivation to engage the West Philadelphia community and commit to its redevelopment.

The success of the university and its president in community engagement has evolved into an ever-growing infrastructure and a mantra of revitalization. Much of this success, however, rests with a small core of individuals with resilient beliefs in democracy and the civic use of higher education. What follows is a discussion of Penn's university–community relations through the perspectives of several key informants regarding the university's structure and its internal political climate and the historical events that led to the West Philadelphia Initiatives.

The information here is based on seven interviews with Penn administrators and staff who are familiar with the university's inner workings and its efforts in West Philadelphia. These informants represent various stakeholder groups. Each also possesses some understanding of who the institutional and extra-institutional stakeholders might be. I do not name these informants, as I agreed to provide them as much anonymity possible. In the case of Ira Harkavy, his role at the university and in its relations with West Philadelphia is too pivotal and central to my argument for him remain anonymous. As I will discuss later, this is both an asset and a liability. Some of the information in this chapter comes directly from confidential memos and other materials shared with me during these interviews.

An analysis of the university's stance toward civic/urban engagement must begin with an analysis of the university's resources in its university–community relations. The most central of these resources is the latest and most enduring of its kind, Penn's Netter Center for Community Partnerships. While the Netter Center is not the absolute authority for urban revitalization, it is a focal point for all of Penn's university–community relations, and its philosophy and staff have influenced the university's engagement with and efforts in West Philadelphia in virtually every way. It became clear through the interviews that the enterprise of university–community relations has been duplicated and fostered in so many different corners of the university that it is impossible for the Netter Center to control or even influence the work of various faculty members, groups, and administrative units. The university, too, recognizes that service-learning programs are not enough to combat the structural sources of urban decline.

Given the current and political nature of some of the qualitative data presented, it is useful to obscure the identities of all informants described in this section of the book with the notable exception of the Netter Center's director, Ira Harkavy. Three of the six anonymous informants are faculty members engaged in studying or connecting their academic interests to the university's efforts in West Philadelphia, or both.

Like many comparable institutions, Penn engaged in its university–community partnerships in order to respond to the demands of many vocal faculty and students, as well as community members who felt that some form of service and reparations were due to them in the wake of the university's involvement in the Urban Renewal projects of the 1960s and 1970s. The rapid deindustrialization of Philadelphia that created blight in West Philadelphia and other areas of the city in many ways created a justification for the university's first large-scale attempts at comprehensive campus planning and real estate development. As some have noted, the expansion and development of the West Philadelphia campus was also driven by the university's desire to join the ranks of Stanford and MIT as part of the Cold War science-military complex.[22]

Harkavy offers a possibly related reason for the university's engagement with its surrounding community—a desire to create a niche, both academic and other, that would distinguish it while making the campus a safer and more attractive place. The following quote from Harkavy firmly locates Penn's interests in West Philadelphia as not in the communities it now serves but in improving its standing within a larger realm of research universities.

Bill Whyte came [in the 1960s,] . . . and he was asked by the senior vice president under Sheldon [Hackney], how you beat Harvard. He said, ". . . you'll never beat Harvard by being Harvard. You'll always be Avis to their Hertz. You do what you, Ira [Harkavy], and . . . these other people are trying to do. You create an intellectual niche and you make that what makes you great, and it's something important. This is the way to do it." What Bill was saying was about comparative advantage . . . and locational advantage, and intellectual advantage.[23]

Harkavy explained that, after hearing Whyte's comments, many Penn leaders and supporters wanted to see the university leverage its resolution of the burgeoning crisis in West Philadelphia as a way of distinguishing the institution. Harkavy's remarks broaden the university's use of its mantra of enlightened self-interest. They refer not only to an attempt to create a safer, cleaner, and more attractive campus but to an attempt to engage in far more ambitious institution building.

There are and have been many people—faculty, administrators, and staff—pushing for Penn's improvement. This is perhaps where the roots of the university's philosophical rifts lie. While Penn's recent successes would appear to have been the work of a great many groups and people functioning in relative harmony, there are actually several significant ideological and methodological divides present within the institution. These are not about *whether* to grow the institution but *how* to grow it and for what purposes.

In addition to Harkavy, two administrators were repeatedly mentioned in some of the interviews to characterize one of the differences in approach and philosophy. The first was John Fry, the university's executive vice president between 1995 and 1999, who charted a course for aggressive, corporate-style campus development. During his tenure, he supervised many of the university's auxiliary functions, such as campus planning and real estate services. Also mentioned in many of the interviews was Jack Shannon, Fry's deputy and associate vice president for special projects. Shannon assisted Rodin and Fry in managing many of the university's high-level and strategic civic relationships with West Philadelphia and the city of Philadelphia at large as well as the larger metropolitan region and its commercial sector.

Several of the informants interviewed made their opinions quite clear that Fry and Shannon were both dynamic and committed institution builders, virtually always in agreement with constituencies such as the Netter Center for Community Partnerships in the belief that a better West Philadelphia would translate into a better university. Shannon was often heard to repeat the mantra "We do well by doing good." The Fry/Shannon camp was often at odds with the Harkavy camp on the end goal and the process that would lead to it. Harkavy summed up his relationship with Fry in this way:

> We both wanted to improve Penn, but clearly my goals were much more related to improving the quality of life in all of West Philadelphia—democratic processes. I think John cared about the development of Penn and that was it. I don't think he'd disagree with that. . . . I think the issue was that my issue

with them was never overt, and I think that the conflicts, if they existed, were over emphasis, style, and my critiquing things at times—that, well, not with John. I wouldn't do this with Jack [Shannon]. I would do it with John—things that he didn't agree with. We battled over the new school. He wanted it to be a private school initially. You know, there were issues.

And I don't know; I think that we had tensions over orientation and goals, but it was never an overt battle. . . . Our goals were different for what Penn should look like within West Philadelphia and within society. I'm not corporatist. I write against commodification. John believes strongly in the commercializing orientation . . . of the universities! He would call students customers. I thought that was blasphemy. He represents a strand within higher education today. This isn't anti-John; it's an orientation. When I was a kid, we used to say, "It's not the person; it's the system." He represents an orientation, goals that are legitimate and distinctly different from my personal goals, which are historically legitimate.

Harkavy's statement is an example of the corporate versus democratic ideal of higher education. It also points to the commodification of higher education and research versus the enterprise of higher learning and knowledge production for social purposes.[24] What makes the University of Pennsylvania such an interesting case is that the individuals involved have also been leaders in these issues nationally. In that way, then, Penn's experience becomes tied to broader disciplinary discourses on university leadership, development, university–community relations, curriculum development, and so on.

One dominant theme of virtually all of the interviews was an analysis of the Rodin presidency. Rodin's tenure saw a marked improvement in the tone of the university's relationship with its West Philadelphia neighbors, as well as with the city's political and civic leadership and its commercial constituencies. However, the credit for such improvement belongs, to one degree or another, to each Penn president since Martin Meyerson (1970–1981). It would appear that every president, including Meyerson's predecessor Gaylord Harnwell (1953–1970), attempted to push the institution in the direction of engagement.

Earlier research reveals that Harnwell did attempt to make amends with Penn's West Philadelphia neighbors but not often in public view.[25] The sum of his attempts could not outweigh the perceived and real damage Penn and the Philadelphia Urban Redevelopment Authority were doing through the displacement of 666 families in the development of the University City Science Center in 1964.[26] However, where Meyerson and Hackney failed, Rodin succeeded and Gutmann has thrived. The credibility of the president's imprimatur is based not on his or her authority but on a relationship between community engagement and the university's academic mission. Gutmann set the tone for her approach to community engagement by starting her inauguration day at a local school wearing a T-shirt and jeans. While the West Philadelphia Initiatives did come to a quiet end, Gutmann's approach to engagement has been no less inclusive than Rodin's.

Sheldon Hackney (1981–1993), the university's sixth president, created the entity that would become the Netter Center for Community Partnerships, which Harkavy now directs in 2011. The Netter Center was originally located in the School of Arts and Sciences (SAS) but reported directly to the president. There was an attempt in the beginning to have it also report to the provost, but the sitting provost's reluctance made this difficult. Harkavy explained that the center's original charge was to be "a university-wide structure designed to bring together the range of university resources to improve the quality of life at Penn and in West Philadelphia."

What Hackney created with the Netter Center was an institutional momentum for complete institutional change. It became clear from all seven interviews, however, that it took four presidencies; numerous student and faculty murders, muggings, rapes, and other nefarious incidents; and drops in admissions standards and selectivity for the university to take the issue of West Philadelphia seriously. Under Hackney, the center first took form in 1983 as the Office of Community Oriented Policy Studies (OCOPS). In the view of one informant, this was a peripheral entity that reported directly to the president but lacked influence on campus.

> Hackney provided some leverage that was more than symbolic. As the program became more popular with faculty, as more faculty and Ira [Harkavy] and Lee [Benson] invented that apt phrase "academically based community service," . . . people began to say, "Well, this is a better way to do teaching, and I can even do research." But especially teaching— making it more exciting, tapping into where kids are, and so forth. From roughly the mid-eighties up until the end of the early nineties, this thing was growing incrementally on campus.

This informant attributed a large part of this "thing" to the faculty's obsession with research and research productivity. He dubs it the "publish, publish, publish, me, me, me, self-aggrandizing pathological faculty" mentality. The struggle to place OCOPS under a high university office and to create a bridge between it and the faculty is one that continues to this day. However, leading up to the West Philadelphia Initiatives, that struggle proved essential to raising the profile of public service within the university and to converting the most recalcitrant faculty, administrators, and students.

In many ways, the departure of a provost not long after Rodin's arrival cleared the way for a new group to recast the OCOPS office as something much larger.[27] Unfortunately, Rodin's arrival was also marked by a chain of incidents that included the death of one doctoral student (1994); the Sled murder in 1996; and a series of dramatic and deadly fires, robberies, and rapes. These incidents created a sense of "fed-up-ed-ness" on campus and in concerned parents, alumni, and trustees.

One informant who was in close contact with Rodin during these times described Rodin's decision to make community engagement central to her presidency. Rodin, a West Philadelphia native, grew up in a solidly middle-class, predominantly Jewish neighborhood that had experienced a significant amount of decline since the 1960s.

Around 1995, there was mounting pressure from various groups on campus for the university to intervene to protect its faculty, staff, and, most important, students. It is not clear that all of these groups agreed on methods or ultimate goals, but what is clear is that the faculty was doing more than making decisions about whether to remain in the neighborhoods near campus. Many of Penn's best and brightest faculty and students were beginning to pursue academic posts and admissions at other institutions.

Despite these challenges, some critics suggested that it was inappropriate for the university to intervene in an issue that was beyond its purview. Many others were firmly convinced that the university was the only organization that could do something about the dangers the campus was facing, and would perhaps have to, in the interest of protecting its viability. The only consensus on what to do about West Philadelphia was that the resolution probably would not involve the vast majority of Penn faculty—particularly those in schools that lacked even a remote connection to public service and engagement in their missions or academic focus.

Given that a great deal of crime in the early 1990s was being perpetrated by young people, the improvement of the city's schools became a special focus of Penn's work in West Philadelphia. However, the Graduate School of Education was one of the last to fully embrace the new focus. Still, a number of faculty members saw their work with the distressed Philadelphia schools as an important step toward ending the violence and helplessness of disenfranchised youth in the surrounding West Philadelphia communities. This work did not deal just with the tremendous problem of distressed schools or public safety; it also created an opportunity for Penn to realize Benjamin Franklin's original goals for the university. Others, like Fry and Shannon, saw it as an opportunity to radically transform and enhance the campus and by extension to achieve much broader and ambitious corporate-style institutional management.

Even with a great deal of interest and demand for university engagement, the then newly installed provost, Stanley A. Chodorow, gave little academic merit to the work of community partnerships and fully expected that they would simply disappear in time. Harkavy and his allies found that a large part of the work of converting faculty and others to their way of thinking involved "proselytizing," not only on the importance of the partnerships themselves but on the use of knowledge and knowledge production for social purposes and of transforming their pedagogy toward that orientation.

One informant provided a great deal of historical perspective on this issue and offered the Wharton School and the Graduate School of Education as examples. The choice of these two schools is interesting in that both were, and still are to some extent, at different ends of the power and influence spectrum among Penn's professional schools and colleges. Wharton, flush with resources, including a current $125 million endowment, wields an inordinate amount of influence over campus affairs and the university's direction. Its position on other university affairs aside, it does now and always has disdained and detached itself from academically based service learning, the university's West Philadelphia Initiatives, and to some extent the city of Philadelphia at large.[28]

The Graduate School of Education, which was originally opposed to the idea of civic engagement, has come a great distance in supporting the work of Harkavy and the Netter Center for Community Partnerships. This informant described his interactions with the dean of the Graduate School of Education:

> My dean here . . . thought it was committing academic suicide . . . getting involved in this kind of stuff . . . or at least tenure suicide. In fact, in the Ed[ucation] School, in 1993, as I recall, when we did our strategic plan, I stood up and said if we don't address West Philadelphia, we're going to be sorry as an institution. In that entire report, that was the only statement about community involvement in the Ed School. . . .
> As I recall, Ira and [another professor] actually came to the dean and asked him to lead this whole initiative. . . . He didn't see this as a very good thing. He was engulfed in a dilemma that the Ed School was badly in the red. It had no endowment to speak of, and no board of trustees or overseers, and couldn't get involved, although I suspect that he would have

given this much greater energy if he had recognized it as something that was going to be developed into [what it has become].

This informant further theorized that many faculty members, particularly younger ones, found Ira's interest in their work to be an unnecessary encroachment and a possible threat to their academic freedom. In most cases, they ultimately became allies of the Netter Center once they ceased viewing it and its philosophy as endangering their intellectual fiefdoms. The Graduate School of Education now actively supports the Penn-assisted K–8 Penn-Alexander School, which has become one of the centerpieces of the University's success in West Philadelphia.

Almost simultaneously, as Rodin herself was increasingly convinced that community engagement would become a central project of her presidency, a newly appointed vice president for government and community relations devised a plan to change the Netter Center's relationship to higher administration. At a conference in California, a group of Penn faculty and administrators drafted a proposal to expand the Netter Center. They subsequently began a national search for a director while solidifying its strategic structural location within the university. Although there are some discrepancies from different voices in the Netter Center's history, there is agreement about moving OCOPS from a peripheral location in the School of Arts and Sciences and instituting direct reporting to the president and the vice president for government and community relations. There was also a new "soft report" to the provost that launched a new era in Penn–West Philadelphia relations. In these ways, the president's office's imprimatur was simultaneously broadened and strengthened, giving it the ability to leverage the president's status as head of the university to draw various university units and faculties into its efforts.

Two informants, including Harkavy, expressed the idea that community partnerships needed tethering to the president and the provost. Their view was that the relationship of the Netter Center to both continues to be critically important for creating greater interest among the university's most important constituency—the faculty. Harkavy said, "It's because structurally, the best thing is to be both [in] an academic and in an administrative capacity that could speak to the entire campus." Having community partnerships connected to the provost not only provided the entire enterprise with a particular credibility with faculty; it also created a basis for maintaining the partnerships beyond some achievable, short-term goal, such as decreased crime and "elegantly" executed campus expansion. Harkavy's perspective was that tying the university's primary business—academics—to its civic engagements ensures that Penn's commitment to the larger project of community development will be sustained for the foreseeable future.

Given Penn's long and contentious history with West Philadelphia, it is easy to assume that the most ardent opposition to its community engagement efforts would have come from the communities themselves. Ironically, this was one of the least discussed topics in this set of interviews. Comments by community residents revealed that most were not and still are not privy to the complexity of the philosophical and practical rifts between university administrators; nor were they privy to the details of the West Philadelphia Initiatives.

As additional groups and stakeholders became interested and involved in urban revitalization in West Philadelphia, the Netter Center's influence faded somewhat. Ira Harkavy had created a set of guiding principles for university civic engagement and service that eventually evolved into the West Philadelphia Initiatives themselves. What he could not have predicted was how various university-based stakeholders would adopt and in some cases adapt those principles for their own purposes. Following is a discussion of some of the university-based stakeholders and the ways they were connected to the philosophy and development of the Netter Center for Community Partnerships.

Without an involved and supportive central administration, the urban engagement project of the university would fail. At most, it would be what it was during and before the Hackney administration (1981–1993)—something that a few faculty members struggled to bring to the attention of the larger institution. Hackney's support and leverage set the stage for Rodin to take the Netter Center in new directions and to greater heights. In response to a question about the Netter Center's future, Harkavy said:

> I could leave Penn, but I don't want to leave Penn. How many years would it take you to build up what I've tried here? One? Two? Three? Penn is the most exciting university in the country for my type of work. There's no one, no place like it. A part of it is because of me, but it's not just because of me. If it weren't for Sheldon [Hackney], weren't for Judy [Rodin], weren't for the people who work for them—and they shall remain nameless—it's me, colleagues, and also leadership, who I may not agree with on everything that they have done, but overall set the right direction.

As stated previously, the imprimatur of the university's chief academic officer proved to be as important as that of the university's chief executive. What was not explicitly discussed during these interviews was the role of scholarship in making the case to faculty—at Penn and beyond. In effect, Harkavy and his peers made the study of successful university–community relations an intellectual endeavor in and of itself. According to one professor:

> Ira's great for Rodin, because she gives him that other piece, that other piece which is good for Penn's image. And he also was contributing, she recognized, [to] the intellectual contribution—the academically based community service in having these problem-focused classes and seminars. She might have seen it as kind of an image thing. And Ira had always said that one of the dangers of being housed in the office of the president, particularly at this university, an elite Ivy League place, is that you'd be co-opted, or the perception of co-optation would exist. If you're being turned into [or] your work is part of the big publicity apparatus, one could speculate that to some extent that's happened, and it's perhaps inevitable. We're good for Penn's public relations.

These remarks also highlight the critical importance of the president's connection to the Netter Center for Community Partnerships for the management of both the university's and the president's image. The relationship between the president and the Netter Center is mutually beneficial. Without it, the university—and the president—lack the ability to fend off criticisms that Penn has acted badly toward the community in one way or another. When compared to Columbia University's evolving debacle in Manhattanville, Penn appears to have many assets that Columbia lacks.[29]

During Rodin's tenure, all of the auxiliary departments related to the university's physical infrastructure—for campus planning, design, construction, real estate development, physical plant and maintenance, and landscaping—were brought together in the same office. The culture of each department was reoriented to the comprehensive campus plan, to greater public participation in planning and design, to Harkavy's five "guiding principles" for improving both Penn and West Philadelphia, and to the work and operations of the other departments in this reorganization. Harkavy's principles—clean and safe streets, quality housing, economic opportunity, public education improvement, and increased retail options—provided structure to the university's efforts as well as avenues of involvement for various university units and constituencies. In this way, these auxiliary departments were able to garner greater financial and administrative support from the university. They were also able to leverage a particular level of legitimacy and social capital that they had not been able to wield before.

As yet unmentioned are constituencies that may be as critically important to the success of university–community relations and the shifts in institutional culture that facilitate them. These are the alumni, trustees, and financial supporters. Obviously these groups are not mutually exclusive, and the most prominent members of each constituency may serve the university in all three ways. They not only support the president but are also the most able to challenge him or her should they disagree with the president's agenda.

At Penn, this cultural shift within the university did not occur only in its administrative units but in the academic units as well. The "publish-or-perish" paradigm in the past ruled and continues to rule Penn's academic culture. What Penn did that few other institutions have done is make service learning appealing to academic departments that typically do not engage in such work. Harkavy and his academic colleagues created a credible argument, buttressed by their interest in action research and their collaborations with others such as Whyte, that service learning can be academically based. Harkavy's argument offered to revolutionize teaching as well as research. Without changing university policies on tenure and promotion, advocates of this type of research made service learning palatable to faculty who were ideologically aligned with this advocacy but more concerned with their own job prospects than with the challenges facing the institution—and, more important, the communities beyond campus.

The strongest motivating factor for many of the constituencies mentioned in this section was not a desire simply to improve the campus as an end unto itself. In Penn's case, the public safety crisis of the early to mid-1990s trumped the institution's historical instinct to engage in institution building in an attempt to "beat Harvard." In this case, that notion simply wasn't enough to spur such a significant proportion of the institution's disparate constituencies to action. Each informant I interviewed who had been affiliated with Penn for more than five years had a crime-related horror story of some kind, including being caught in the midst of a shootout. The crime factor was important because it discouraged students from active participation in city life. Just as important, it dampened the spirit of the campus.

An important lesson from the Penn case is that any successful attempt to engage urban communities requires a nonpresidential advocate and manager. Harkavy has remained the best person for the job at Penn because of his work in West Philadelphia as a student and his sustained friendships with numerous members of the West Philadelphia community. He has brought to the position legitimacy and energy, from which the university has benefited handsomely. One informant said this about Harkavy and his job:

Hey, it's vital to your existence. He's been that way. He has alliances out the kazoo—churches, business, and political organizations—and he just knows how to work. . . . His contacts and his understanding and his understanding of university culture—the social situation, the social forces—really ha[ve] credibility. He has credibility because he delivers on his promises. And it's the charisma—and he is [charismatic]—and I don't necessarily mean that when you're in a room, everyone gravitates towards him, but he does have a way of mobilizing people around ideas.

The process of recruiting and converting faculty from wary careerists to community advocates/pedagogical revolutionaries is tough and often thankless work. Harkavy's ability to do this had much to do with where faculty members were intellectually located within the university and how their bodies of work spoke for them, both on campus and beyond. He was clear that his standing as an academic had much to do with the strength and level of support he received from the administrator he primarily reported to, the dean of the School of Arts and Sciences (SAS). At Penn, this is one of the largest and most powerful schools. Its former dean and former chair of the sociology department, Sam Preston, has been allied with Harkavy and his work in West Philadelphia almost from the start. His appointment as dean of the School of Arts and Sciences, his individual reputation as a scholar and colleague, and his relationship to Harkavy only enhanced the Netter Center's legitimacy and its appeal to a wider faculty audience.

The Netter Center's success confronts the institution with one specific and tremendous challenge, according to this informant:

I keep telling him [Harkavy], "Cross streets in Philadelphia very carefully, Ira. If you get killed, the gig's up. We're out of business." My worry about this [institutional charisma, beyond Harkavy] is that I don't think we have it. I think that that's acknowledged. They don't want to hear it, maybe. There's nobody in the wings that can lead this thing, in my judgment.

The Netter Center for Community Partnerships and Ira Harkavy himself have enjoyed the support of a cast of characters, including those from the highest levels within the university. As the administration changed hands from Rodin to Gutmann in 2004, a number of the Netter Center's most ardent supporters (and their counterparts on what remains of the John Fry/profit-oriented side of the issue) departed. As with every major administrative transition, the Netter Center finds itself vying for position among other priorities and interests. Fortunately, the success of the past fifteen years, as reported by my informants in this chapter, suggests that the rationale for sustaining the West Philadelphia project into the near future remains sound.

The interviews in this chapter represent only a cursory examination of the inner workings of the university. What this analysis may offer is a clear way of identifying the philosophical differences that exist between factions in the university's leadership, faculty, and staff. Given the strength of Penn's corporate orientation, there is a shared impression among my informants here that perhaps the work of university–community relations can be co-opted. The university president lends the work his or her imprimatur but in return may require the project's cooperation or deployment for other purposes. In response to my question of whether or not Harkavy feels deployed, he says, "I try to avoid being deployed. There are times when I know that our good work allows certain things to happen. I also know that because we allow certain things to happen, our good work grows and develops, and we're able to do better things."

Harkavy clearly sees this as "acceptable compromises" made in the name of the greater good of the university and the West Philadelphia community. One informant offered a contrasting view, in which co-optation may be unavoidable but much easier to agree to if compromises have already been struck. However, the compromises themselves may not always yield what had been hoped from them. The following statement from Harkavy demonstrates how his optimism may blind him to the realities of opportunities for co-optation and acquiescence.

My sense is that they think that they understand where we're situated. They understand it's an institution. They understand what we stand for. They understand what Penn is standing more and more for. And they also understand that often at times we are utilized as somewhat of a cover, but we are also able to play and do things the next day.

Harkavy and other informants were also clear that the Netter Center's philosophy and work are threatened not only by competing interests from without but by mission creep from within. The compromises that Harkavy and his staff make to maintain the center's position within the university consistently challenge their ability to steer university–community partnerships away from the university's corporate interests. On that subject, Harkavy was resolute in stating that he is willing to make some compromises to reach the goal of an institution that is ruled by a democratic ideology. Had he not been willing to make compromises on where the center would be located, the reporting structure that governs it, and the nature of its work, it probably would have died long before Rodin arrived on campus. Harkavy himself admits that the challenge is to remain consistently focused on the best interests of both the target communities and the university and to organize the Netter Center's work so that the compromises he is forced to make on its behalf do not outweigh that work.

One last potential weakness in this model is that the university partnerships—writ large—may become so ubiquitous that accountability will suffer. Versions of Harkavy's West Philadelphia model of academically based service learning are now operating in virtually every university academic and administrative unit in some form or fashion. More important, they now work alongside and, at some points, in opposition to the Netter Center. Rodin provided the center with a place of honor that made the other efforts peripheral even if they actually had greater fiscal or staff resources. In my interview with Harkavy, he gave Rodin a great deal of credit and praise for what Penn accomplished in the ten years between her inauguration and her departure.

With Rodin gone and Gutmann, a nonnative Philadelphian now at the helm, a good deal of work will have to be done to replicate what Rodin and Harkavy created together. An even larger challenge is maintaining Penn's institutional momentum in various areas. While Harkavy's optimism and dedication to the project are inspiring, it may be difficult, if not impossible, to find a successor who can sustain this momentum for very long. This presents Penn and other institutions seeking to duplicate Penn's success with a problem. Virtually all of the things that the university was able to do in the past ten years were related to the Netter Center for Community Partnerships, its charismatic director, and the goodwill that he has banked on behalf of the Netter Center, which is simultaneously his and Penn's. In the end, the center's continued success will depend on its ability to institutionalize its philosophy while negotiating its co-existence with competing interests within and beyond the university.

The Ascendance of University-Driven Real Estate Development

Under Rodin's leadership, the university's Real Estate Services office became spatially and operationally attached to the Campus Planning, University Architect, Facilities Management, and Development Offices. I conducted a structured interview with members of the Real Estate Services team along with a Penn staff member who was intimately involved in campus planning and real estate investing. My analysis here is informed by both this interview and other interviews that overlapped with this subject. The excerpts that follow focus on two aspects of the university's real estate development strategy. The primary interest is in the pressures that influence this strategy and the methods by which the strategic goals are reached.

More important than profit generation, the focus of the University Architect, the Campus Planning and Physical Plant staffs, and Real Estate Services is to serve the university's various constituencies. The Penn faculty is a key constituency. As stated elsewhere in this book, competition for talented faculty is intense among elite schools. Providing them with the necessary facilities and amenities is critical in these contests. One interviewee noted:

> As [the] faculty change—I hate to call them acquisitions—but [consider] this professor from Hopkins, Dr. Smith [name changed]. What if I need more space, and that contradicts what I told you I needed two years ago? That's exactly what happened with both Dr. Smith and [Dr.] Johnson. Smith was hired, and they basically said, "Congratulations, here are your terms and conditions." And then they said, "Oh gosh, where are we gonna house him?" After he had signed and accepted the letter, we got this call: "What can we do?" What about this Translational Research building? He opened [his lab] last week. He moved right in. His vision is when we get the Skircanage, which is our bioengineering building that's up on the engineering campus, built. It's a little tiny thing that's right in there. That's all engineering buildings.

I asked about how often Penn "acquires" faculty. Such an enterprise would mean that the university possesses a storehouse of properties that it saves for just such situations.

> HFE: Did you own it the whole time? Is it something that you acquired, too?

> Penn staffer: We didn't know why we acquired it; we just acquired it. It was a former machine-equipment repair building—very heavy industrial use for Westinghouse. They remanufactured engines, electric motors, and transformers. So we bought the building in 1999, really without too much strategy. We just figured, "You know what? We're going to need it."

> HFE: How much land banking do you do?

> Penn staffer: We do a lot. We're constantly looking. Look at the history, the Post Office [Annex]. We have tried for almost

thirty-five years to acquire that property. I can go back. I inherited this box of correspondence. I should send it to the archives. For thirty-five years, Penn has communicated with the Post Office about acquiring this tract of land that's south of Walnut. It's fourteen acres. It's just a natural land-banking growth. We finally got the deal done. It's pure land banking— because Penn grows about fifty acres every seventy-five years.

The Post Office Annex to which the staff member referred was transferred to the university in 2005 by the U.S. Post Office, which relocated much of its mail distribution from Thirtieth, Market, and Chestnut Streets to a new facility in southwest Philadelphia. The transfer allowed Penn to put in a bid to the city for the parcels of the first post office site. In the months that followed the announcement of the land transfer, a series of meetings were held to garner Penn community feedback on proposed plans for an eastward campus expansion. The university's intentions are to do more than simply enlarge the campus; the expansion will also allow it to face the central business district by having campus buildings and facilities sit along the banks of the Schuylkill River.

One of my key interests in this meeting was to understand how planning decisions are made and how they interface with the WPI. Despite the existence of a comprehensive long-term plan for university growth and development, long-term goals are not explicitly tied to enrollment or space needs projections.

HFE: So, how much land banking happens with the individual parcels outside (west and north)?

Penn staffer: We own properties here and there [*pointing at map on a conference room table*]. And we acquired, I mean, I acquired—the department acquired—a property at Fortieth and Pine, for example. It was an old nursing home. It was disreputable and a really terrible building. We just needed it. We wanted the indigent old-timers that lived there to go somewhere else, because we wanted the operator, who was a very, you know—[he] should have been in jail. We wanted him out. So we bought the building and got them out and are going to redevelop the building. It's a little site. It's a one-acre site. We're doing little things.

HFE: You're going to redevelop it for Penn student housing? Or for what?

Penn staffer: Not sure. Not sure. It could be a lot of things. It could be student housing.

In a related vein, this staffer explained that the eastward expansion and the land-banking activities *are* in some ways tied to master campus plans and the university's interest in revitalizing West Philadelphia.

We repeat the plan like we're saying the pledge of allegiance. This is what we're trying to do. This is not about coming out and building a new thing for a university. This is about economic development. It's about city building. It's about creating connectivity between Center City and the university. It's about being a good neighbor. It's about, you know, creating spaces for our own people—meaning the Dr. Smiths or Dr. Johnsons [names changed] or whatever the future [is] of unnamed doctors doing research in these buildings.

It is also about staying competitive with other top research universities. The "acquisition" of "Dr. Smith" from Hopkins was significant on many levels. Hopkins and Penn maintain an intense but friendly rivalry for being named top university in National Institutes of Health (NIH) research funding. The hiring away of a highly talented researcher directly from Hopkins puts Penn in the lead. As important as NIH ranking is, research commercialization and potential royalties also matter; other researchers may follow the recruited researcher. On this point, the staffer remarked:

We're a support system for this institution. Fundamentally, this is a real estate deal. But it's also called a "build to suit." [In] one of the things that I'm particularly in charge of . . . [Dr. Smith] is also a part of the story."

He says to people, when he goes out to talk about it, "I had courage; I moved from my building, which is in the basement of one of our hospitals—I moved my lab and my people, taking my intellectual capacity to this eastern location. I've got a great state-of-the-art lab. I'm part of the university's eastward momentum. I'm helping to improve the quality of life over here." And frankly, if he splits on us, we could fill that space in a heartbeat.

The goal here is not to ensure that top faculty like "Dr. Smith" remain at Penn. I understand the staffer's remarks to mean that the larger goal is to be ready to accommodate a scientist of his caliber on short notice. So, according to Terino's assessment, Penn and its perpetual effort to chase preeminence among top-tier schools in research productivity started during the Cold War and may continue today.[30] An example of how Penn modeled this was discussed by my informant:

Remember [at] MIT, Millennium Pharmaceutical went from a nothing idea in a researcher over at Whitehead Institute in his lab to being a one-million-square-foot tenant in buildings that MIT owns. And that happened in fifteen years. That could happen here. The Center for Technology Transfer is moving people out. When the Center for Technology Transfer has a success, where do those people go? Cambridge; Menlo Park; Ann Arbor, Michigan; North Carolina; San Diego. They're not here. . . . What we need to do is create an investment environment, and that's what we hope to do out here on fourteen acres where that can happen.

Some of the university's real estate development activities are focused on students and on the end goals of the West Philadelphia

Initiatives themselves. The Penn staffer I spoke with was intimately involved in the Fresh Grocer complex development. Of course, the university does not want to lose money on its investment, but it is able to take risks as a technically tax-exempt institution that a private investor or developer cannot. Moreover, a great deal of the university leadership's urgency may have had something to do with a desire to silence the critics and constituent groups that inspired Penn to engage in the WPI. A confidential draft memo on the West Philadelphia Initiatives from 1995 spoke specifically to the need for a supermarket. On that topic, the staffer shared the following:

> Penn staffer: Well, with the Fresh Grocer, we had a whole community infrastructure in place to say, "Penn has set out to improve Fortieth Street, and this is the centerpiece of our Fortieth Street revitalization strategy." We have some interesting things we own, and it's becoming more widely known. We bought a bunch of really sleazy businesses on the upper Fortieth Street. I call it the upper Fortieth Street. You know, it's between Chestnut, Walnut, or Chestnut to Ludlow and Sansom and Fortieth Street. And these were some crack houses and, you know, a really scary kind of neighborhood business that needed to be [closed down]. Penn was in a hurry.
>
> HFE: Why?
>
> Penn staffer: We had to change the world. If you're going to change the world, you can't [wait].
>
> HFE: But there was a supermarket down the street—?
>
> Penn staffer: It was despicable and very dangerous.
>
> HFE: Was that the rush—to give students another option?
>
> Penn staffer: We had a five-point plan. We needed—you've got Ira's book; you've seen our five-point plan. [1] clean and

safe, [2] neighborhood retail and commercial, [3] housing—
you know, put into place an urban design plan that included
all of the furniture and street trees and make Penn a good
neighbor. Make our buildings better. Make them urban. That
was the five-point plan, and I just skipped over chapters and
chapters of the book. You know, each of those really had a
strategy. But when we did the Fresh Grocer, and the garage,
we adhered to those principles, and that was all about get-
ting neighborhood commercial—the classic neighborhood
commercial—in the grocery store. You can't have a good
residential quality if you don't have a good grocery store, and
we put our bucks on the line to build a grocery store.

The urgent tone of the WPI was nested in Ira Harkavy's language and ideas, but the initiatives were being used to rationalize the
mode and speed of the university's real estate development efforts. At
no point in this, or any other interview, did this staffer or anyone else
besides Harkavy speak about an evolution in the university's mission.
Instead, there was much implied about an evolving culture of a once
sleepy but great Ivy League research university on a quest to use
the crisis of West Philadelphia to reinvigorate its most recalcitrant
constituencies. The enhancement of Penn as a research university,
as a community partner, and as a center for prestige and excellence
was somehow tied to the fate of West Philadelphia. Penn leadership
could marshal its constituencies around this cause for many reasons.
As for residents of West Philadelphia, or staff who spend a great deal
of time there, improvements in retail amenities, public safety, and so
forth benefited them directly through improved services and options
and through their connection to an institution in many ways on an
upward swing.

   Given Penn's historically contentious relationship with its West
Philadelphia neighbors, the question remains why none of this activity generated more protests or resistance. As I would find out from
interviews with area residents, there actually was a great deal of dis-
content in West Philadelphia. The Real Estate Services Office and
others in the Penn administration had learned well from history and

approached the WPI with its community relations infrastructure ready to engage irritated constituencies and support development in whatever ways possible.

The staffer I spoke to offered an apt analogy to explain how the university went about purchasing a set of storefront properties along Fortieth Street as a part of its corridor revitalization program:

> If the university tried to do it, we would fail. And the reason for that is because you're fighting thirty or forty years of animosity. I say it's like a big dog in a small room. The dog is a friendly dog. He really wants to please, but he's a big dog. And he comes in the room and his tails wags and he knocks over the lamp and he doesn't mean to. And everyone around here wants to do the right thing; it's just [that], institutionally, when you get into community development, you can't help yourself.

Like many universities, Penn has learned that its real estate acquisition and development strategy must involve third parties. In most cases, the third parties are capable and legitimate developers, community development corporations, banks, and others with an interest in the success of a particular project or target area. In other cases, they may be chosen because of their shared identities or long-term history with property occupants or sellers. This is particularly true when race is involved. An African American developer may be chosen simply because he or she is seen as being able to reduce any resistance the university (and its partners) might encounter. Still, the benefits of revitalization for long-term residents are there, even if those residents are resistant simply because a project is being driven or supported by the university. One informant explained:

> We're seeing portfolios turn over, where investors that have owned properties for thirty, forty, fifty years are now selling the family assets, and they're getting sixty to seventy-five thousand bucks a unit. I think that's a great thing. I can see already, in the foreground, gentrification might become an

issue. But you take things in stride. You take things in order. And Philadelphia has a long, long way to [go] before this becomes—including almost a million empty homes, a million homes and land that used to accommodate a million people—poof, all gone. So we've got a long, long way to go. But, you know, we've changed the world, and now the market forces are working in our favor.

The ideologies of the corporate and service-oriented faces of the University of Pennsylvania may not be as operationally divided as individuals who are involved may like to think. A contradictory, symbiotic relationship exists between the two that involves many more actors and constituent groups (or those acting in their stead) than I could interview. The West Philadelphia Initiatives took shape with significant contributions from the Netter Center for Community Partnerships, but they did not fit into Penn's real estate development strategy. As a planning exercise, the West Philadelphia Initiatives exposed the ideological divides within the university, and their impacts are yet unfolding.

3

Early Returns on Dramatic
Efforts to Change

The West Philadelphia Initiatives, 1990–2005

On October 21, 1994, Judith Rodin walked into her inauguration and into history as Penn's seventh president, after a distinguished twenty-year career in higher education. She returned to Penn as the first woman president of an Ivy League institution. Rodin's return to Philadelphia was also significant because it was a homecoming to the section of the city where she had been raised. Stories in the *Philadelphia Inquirer* and the *Daily Pennsylvanian*, as well as some university announcements, suggest that Rodin's realization that her tenure would be about resolving the "West Philadelphia problem" came only after a series of high-profile crimes on and around the Penn campus in the mid-1990s, but there is evidence that refutes this suggestion. In her inaugural speech, Rodin stated:

> Philadelphia is my hometown. I first came to Penn three decades ago, wide-eyed, only because of a precious scholarship for local students. Returning here, I find special meaning and emotion in so many of each day's rituals and experiences. . . .

I have no doubt that this city, despite its problems, is one of Penn's greatest blessings. It is central to the Penn experience—not a world apart. I intend to work every day that I am here, as both a personal and an institutional mission, with community leaders and public officials, with our schools and health clinics, on things both large and small, to enhance the relationship in ways that will enrich both Penn and Philadelphia. We are, and must be, truly one.[1]

During my research, a Penn staffer I spoke with shared copies of administrative memos and reports given to Rodin and other senior university administrators regarding Penn's impending action plan for West Philadelphia. In one briefing paper from March 1994, nearly eight full months before her inaugural, I identified five priority issues that required attention: (1) safety, (2) jobs, (3) economic and commercial development, (4) quality of public education, and (5) health care. The report geographically separated West Philadelphia into two areas with different populations, challenges, and priorities. The first area was an "inner ring" that was (and is) more racially and economically diverse than the "outer ring" that was (and remains) more homogenous and predominantly African American. The briefing paper speaks specifically to the university's activities and to a clear rationale for urban engagement—self-interest.

In late November 1994, a much more detailed draft report, "Strategy and Actions for West Philadelphia Plan," provided more information about specific opportunities for engagement and steps to be taken by the university to take advantage of them. While jobs, public education, and health care were still a part of this second report, they were much less prominent. In their place, economic and commercial development—particularly along distressed retail corridors—was described as a critical piece of West Philadelphia's urban revitalization. The report differed from both its predecessor and later drafts about the West Philadelphia plan by its lack of hubris about the university's capabilities and by referencing opportunities to partner or support the work of local organizations in their community development/urban revitalization projects.

The last pre–West Philadelphia Initiatives (WPI) report I un-
covered was a draft prepared for the university in November 1996,
which most closely resembled what actually took place between
1994 and 2004. It called for improvements in commercial and economic development, housing, and general quality of life and educational opportunities for children. The total proposed cost at that
time was more than $10 million. Those funds would be used in a
variety of ways, including the construction of a new public school
and a supermarket, a public safety effort, and property acquisition
and rehabilitation.

In the end, the WPI proved to be larger and more expansive
than any draft report had proposed. As a result, "buckets" of activity were defined to organize disparate (and possibly contradictory)
efforts across and beyond the university. To that end, five major strategic objectives or themes were identified: (1) clean and safe streets,
(2) excellent school options, (3) high-quality housing options,
(4) reinvigorated retail, and (5) increased job opportunities. Many of
the participants in this study cited Ira Harkavy, the well-known director of the Netter Center for Community Partnerships as the source
of these ideas. However, there were other segments of the Penn
community, including Penn Faculty and Staff for Neighborhood
Issues (PFSNI), that had become very concerned about the rise in
crime around the campus and had publicly outlined their wishes for
an engaged university.[2]

Many of my informants understood that on some levels Penn
was able to make significant strides in its revitalization effort largely
because of the coalescing of various trends and factors that contributed to the university's progress. This chapter focuses on three components of the university's West Philadelphia Initiatives that were
most often cited as significant drivers of change in University City
and West Philadelphia. As stated in Chapter 1, this book is not intended to be a comprehensive evaluation of the initiatives. As significant contributors to urban neighborhood change in University City,
however, they do warrant description and analysis. The two components that are not discussed are those that had missions that my
informants either did not know about or did not care to discuss. My

view of the relatively scant discussion of those components—public safety and economic inclusion—is that most informants believed and expected that Penn would play a significant role in crime reduction because crime was the issue that launched the WPI. Economic inclusion was developed later in the process and was not well known among many people either within or beyond the university.

What follows should not be read as an alternative interpretation of the facts laid out in Kromer and Kerman's WPI report.[3] That report was a balanced and comprehensive review of the rationale behind the WPI and a plainly written account of positive Penn-driven change in West Philadelphia. Instead, my analysis briefly restates what is publicly known about the WPI and provides some analysis of the WPI's impacts based on data generated from interviews with West Philadelphians.

Housing

Based on Harkavy's guidelines, improving housing became central to the West Philadelphia Initiatives. Stabilizing the neighborhood in many ways depended on the university's ability to lure middle-class residents and ultimately their own students back to the area. The challenges of the area's housing supply were obvious even to the most casual observers. The three major components of Penn's strategy are summarized here.

Mortgage Programs

Residents believe that this component of the initiatives, known popularly and simply as "Penn's mortgage program," has had a great effect on home values and neighborhood composition. The history of the university's support of employee homeownership is actually much longer than the history of the initiatives. Since the 1960s, the university has been guaranteeing mortgages for employees. However, it was not until the initiatives were adopted that more banks were added to the program to increase the competitiveness of interest rates and the program was better marketed to Penn faculty and staff.

The success of the "revived" program inspired Penn faculty and staff to live much further west than many had ever considered before. The character of many blocks was changed by the presence of often highly educated and white or foreign-born faculty and staff. In some cases, these beneficiaries of the mortgage program assimilated well into the social fabric of their new neighborhoods, while others isolated themselves from intricate social networks based on the geography of block/neighborhood associations.

The program consists of two parts. The older part, the Guaranteed Mortgage Program, is structured to provide mortgages to full-time Penn employees seeking to buy homes within a defined portion of West Philadelphia. As it evolved, the coverage area was expanded to include more of West Philadelphia as well as additional banks with higher mortgage guarantees to provide capital for renovations. The newer part of the program provides cash to aid with closing costs and mortgage fees. Both segments were designed exclusively to assist full-time university faculty and staff. The guarantee amount was reduced in 2004 from $15,000 to $7,500 to make the program available to a greater number of employees. The program has since been renamed the Forgivable Loan Program and is administered by the Penn Home Ownership Services Office.

A notable anecdote on the program is that it has not been accessible exclusively to full-time faculty and staff of the university. Throughout its history, there have been occasions when people other than Penn employees or affiliates were able to pursue homeownership through Penn's programs.

The "Fund"

Through the capitalization of an endowment in partnership with a private developer, the university created a $5 million fund (known as the "Fund") to acquire and renovate apartment buildings close to the university campus. The goal was to create a larger pool of nearby market-rate housing for students and to rid neighborhoods of the crime-ridden buildings that housed hundreds of poor and transient residents.

In all, five large buildings between Fortieth and Fiftieth Streets were renovated. Their average rent, before the Fund acquired and renovated them, for a one-bedroom apartment was $550 per month in the 1999–2000 academic year. The average for the same size apartment in 2004–2005 was $670.

Tenants were not evicted or relocated during the renovation. As residents terminated leases and relocated out of a building, upgrades were made to individual units. The modest increases in rent do not reflect the perception that rents skyrocketed in West Philadelphia as a result of the initiatives. Instead, the number of lower-cost options was reduced by other landlords who made substantial improvements to their own buildings (independent of any assistance from the university) in order to have their building "acquired" by Penn via the Fund and so obtain a higher price at sale. When the university opted not to purchase several buildings, landlords kept rents high to recoup their losses and match competing services and rental prices.

Vacant Home Rehabilitation

Another effort initiated by the university at this time was the acquisition and rehabilitation of persistently vacant housing in the University City neighborhoods. A small team of Penn officials traveled the streets of West Philadelphia—on foot—exploring the area's persistently vacant and decrepit homes. The goal was to identify long-term vacancies for acquisition, renovation, and sale. Given the architecture of Philadelphia's housing stock, one or more long-term vacancies could potentially destroy the aesthetic quality of a block of homes and contribute to the idea that the area was blighted and neglected—even if it was not.

Between 1998 and 2002, nineteen homes were acquired and renovated using university funds. The homes were then sold on the private market. The renovation costs in many cases exceeded the prices that the homes were able to fetch. According to some Penn officials, prices were not a reflection of the university's poor management of the property renovations or failure to select appropriate properties but were rather the sign of a market that had not caught up with demand. A former Penn staffer intimately involved in the housing program shared the following:

> We had houses that didn't even make it to the market. Couples would walk by and ask if the house being worked on was one of the "Penn" houses. We sold one or two before we even listed it. The houses got the reputation in the area for being renovated by good contractors using the best materials.

In the end, the university lost money on these houses, which by several accounts sold for less than $250,000 but cost more than $300,000 to acquire and renovate. This cost to the university was repaid in the increasing stabilization of the area's housing market. The thrust and mission of the project was consistent with other efforts—to allow the university to engage in investments that were too risky or that appeared unattractive to the market and then allow the market to do the rest.

For others, particularly seniors and those on limited incomes, the increased tax assessments encouraged them to consider selling and leaving the area. Many homes increased in value by over 300 percent between the middle 1990s and 2006.[4] Renters have been the most affected. In 1999, the university created a capital fund for the purchase and renovation of several large apartment buildings surrounding the Penn campus. This collaborative effort by the university and a real estate development firm not only made several buildings more appealing to students; it also limited their accessibility to lower-income residents and inspired many other landlords to renovate their buildings as well. The net effect was a steep climb in area rents. Another consequence was the phenomenon of many absentee landlords selling their multiple-unit buildings or converting them into single-family homes and selling them at higher prices. Through the conversions, many renters were either priced out or simply had their leases terminated when they expired. Some renters, including many students, moved west and south in search of cheaper rents, while others took their evictions as an opportunity to purchase homes. Many of those in the best position to do this were Penn employees who took advantage of the Enhanced Mortgage Program.

The 2004 expansion of the program's target area included many neighborhoods where home values had not risen to the point of being beyond the reach of lower-salaried university employees. The movement of renters and new homeowners into these areas unsettled housing patterns in previously homeowner-dominated neighborhoods west and south of University City. The divide between community organizers, homeowners, and renters was clear. Indeed, few of my homeowner informants could name renters to whom they could refer me. A number of the renters I did speak to were students or potential informants who were "struggling" or "working too much," or they were potential drug addicts or what several called "too intense." When I asked about former renters who had moved around University City or out of it, most informants were unable to provide me with contact information or did not follow up on promises to facilitate an introduction.

Retail Development

Several groups worked along with the university to create new retail options. The rationale on all sides was that there was an undiscovered and underexploited market for high-end retail services in the area.[5] Like many other Philadelphia communities, West Philadelphia was underserved by retail amenities. Focus group research conducted by Penn revealed a great demand among area residents and on-campus constituencies. The university directly managed three major projects: (1) the Fresh Grocer, (2) the Bridge: Cinema de Lux, and (3) Sansom Common/University Square.

A fourth retail development owned and managed by the university is a former eatery/office building at the intersection of Thirty-Fourth and Walnut Streets. The Fortieth Street corridor between Walnut and Spruce has been almost entirely upgraded, including additional space on the first floor of the School of Dentistry. There are also new retail developments along Walnut Street on the ground level of the Inn at Penn between Thirty-Sixth and Thirty-Eighth

Streets and between Thirty-Eighth and Fortieth Streets in the Radian building.

The university worked, and continues to work, with community leaders, small business owners, and other interested parties on the rehabilitation of the Fortieth Street, Baltimore Avenue, and Lancaster Avenue retail corridors.

Before 1999, the parcel immediately adjacent to the Annenberg School of Communication, the Annenberg Theatre, the rear of the Van Pelt-Dietrich Library, and the Institute for Contemporary Art was an open parking lot. This central location was a geographical crossroads of the campus and the northernmost face of its contiguous campus core. It was also woefully underutilized as useful space.

One of the jewels in Penn's retail development efforts was University Square. Situated at the corner of Thirty-Sixth and Walnut Streets, the $90 million, 300,000-square-foot complex contains a popular plaza, the Penn bookstore (the largest by square footage in the entire city and managed by Barnes and Noble Booksellers), several high-end retail brand stores, two high-end and noted restaurants, and a Hilton hotel. This was the only project in Penn's portfolio that was financed entirely by the university.

One of the other jewels is the Fresh Grocer complex at the corner of Fortieth and Walnut Streets. For several decades, supermarkets and other food outlets poorly served the neighborhoods of West Philadelphia. Prior to Penn's involvement, the primary supermarket in the area was a Thriftway at the intersection of Forty-Third and Walnut Streets. The popular consensus garnered from interviews was that this store was inexpensive and poorly managed. The meat section often displayed old and fatty meats; the aisles were often crowded with unstocked goods, open palettes, and other debris. Spills and other hazards were often not quickly removed. Given its place as University City's only full-service market, Thriftway was often very crowded and chaotic. Its best feature was its array of international foods that served West Philadelphia's diverse immigrant communities and middle-class tastes.

The university's various outreach offices and a number of community groups attempted to address grievances with the Thriftway operator on several occasions. The operator's perceived reluctance to make improvements prompted the university to draw up plans to either buy out the store and shut it down or construct a new supermarket and drive Thriftway out of business through pure competition. The result is the Fresh Grocer that sits at Fortieth and Walnut, directly across from the university's subsidized entertainment complex. A young squatter who was living in West Philadelphia in various vacant houses shared the following perspective with me:

> I hate that store. It's just this rich bougie[6] place that caters to white people who have too much money. I've stolen stuff from there, which is really easy. They have cameras everywhere, and you can see the security booth and that no one's inside watching the cameras. For some awful reason, they never figured out to put up a one-way mirror to stop people from seeing that no one's watching the cameras.

The Fresh Grocer was aided by the development of a retail entertainment complex on the southwest corner of Fortieth and Walnut that includes a high-end eatery, the Marathon Grill, a high-end movie theater, and, on the second floor, a well-decorated cosmopolitan lounge/bar. The goal of this development was for Penn students to find entertainment directly off campus.

At one dinner meeting, I asked a group of African American former West Philadelphia residents how they felt about some of the new developments, particularly the movie theater. One said, "Yeah, I think that the tickets are like $10.75. That's just a nigga tax. They don't want us up in there. Wasn't that theater supposed to be for the community? Who's going to pay that to see a movie? I'll take my ass to Sixty-Ninth Street."

Nevertheless, the entertainment complex continues to be popular with West Philadelphia teens, who have difficulty traveling to other movie theaters that show first-run movies and new releases (other than the one at Sixty-Ninth Street mentioned by my informant). For most residents, the new retail amenities are convenient and were sorely needed. They are, however, beyond the means of many and perhaps the most public manifestation of the changing neighborhood. More important, the quality of the retail offerings is a symbol of a shifting community identity.

Public Education

Over the past seventy years, the Philadelphia public school system has been one of the nation's most troubled. A state takeover in 2001 facilitated the privatization of several schools and the creation of a slew of new charter schools as well as relationships between existing schools and "educational management organizations" (EMOs).[7] Prior to the takeover, Penn was finalizing plans to create a new school to meet the needs of the communities closest to its campus that it would design and manage itself. Through the takeover process, Penn's memorandum of understanding (MOU) with the Penn-Alexander School made it a university partner, similar to the for-profit corporations that had accepted contracts to run a select number of troubled schools.

This component of the WPI has been reported as successful, but it has also been an incredibly divisive issue pitting neighborhood association against neighborhood association and even neighbors against neighbors and friends against friends. One neighborhood association has done more with Penn than all of the others, leading to a charge of being "in bed" with the university. One year before the university announced plans to establish and support a new neighborhood school, several University City neighborhood associations were sending delegates to a newly formed "Community Council."

Once the plans for the school were announced, one group (the one that would benefit most) withdrew from the Community Council, creating a rift between the neighborhood associations that is still somewhat unresolved. The issue that inspired the rift was the definition of the school's catchments area, which would have limited access to the area where the greatest proportion of Penn faculty and staff lived and that was closest to the university campus itself.

Alternative proposals for a magnet school, an expanded catchments area, or a lottery were rejected by the university outright. The recent release of the school's test scores on state assessments had revealed that they were "disappointingly mediocre." Contrary to many media-driven myths about the school, a good number of students attending it are neither children of the long-term persistently poor nor privileged children of Penn professors. It is in fact a mix of the two groups and several others. Many families of all economic backgrounds crowded into owner- and renter-occupied housing when plans for the school were announced. In some cases, families who rented apartments in the catchments area were "doubling" up on children so that as many as possible could be eligible to attend. This did not, however, dissuade many parents of all races and economic levels from attempting to move into an area that many assumed had one the best run and most resource-rich schools in the entire district. The result was a dramatic increase in sale prices for homes in the school's catchments area.

The university's housing initiatives were varied in both scope and transparency. Many of the university's efforts, such as the Enhanced Mortgage Program, were advertised and well known to the general public. Others, such as the Fund rehabilitation program and the Vacant House Rehabilitation Program, were less well known but significant in their impacts. The sections that follow describe these three major programs and present resident views of their impacts on West Philadelphia neighborhoods. Many resident informants cited major changes in housing prices. At the very least, the marketing of West Philadelphia—or a small part of it—as a neighborhood with a quality public school succeeded.[8]

Community Perspectives on Penn's Work

"Penn should give itself a passing grade. Although it may be a leader among its peers in this regard, it still has quite a long way to go." —West Philadelphia resident

How can one university undo nearly a century of urban social isolation, racism, the residue of inadequate social services and public infrastructure, and persistent poverty? If it wanted to, would it even be possible? Consider patterns of disinvestment and decline that extend well beyond Penn's circle of influence. Penn is a wealthy, large, exclusive institution situated in a contested urban terrain that will most likely draw criticism regardless of the initiatives it undertakes. It represents both the exclusion of many from the best the American educational system has to offer and the best opportunity for them to gain access to another social and economic station in life.

Penn's decision to engage in urban revitalization was based on the idea that West Philadelphia had reached an unacceptable state of crisis. This may have had more to do with the real dangers of West Philadelphia than it did with the inability or unwillingness of Penn students, faculty, and staff to navigate an urban environment that was becoming increasingly hostile generally—but also increasingly hostile to Penn's broadened sense of entitlement and race/class privilege. How white or black was West Philadelphia in actuality?

Questions about the university inspired a variety of responses. They were for the most part positive, with many residents expressing gratitude for its efforts. Still, many informants were skeptical of the university's interests, citing their perception of its current withdrawal of investment and effort. One resident of more than thirty years felt that the university's efforts were cyclical. Once a crisis ended, priorities shifted and disinvestment restarted. Myths about Penn's interests abound and are endlessly scintillating. These myths are often in conflict with the university's stated interests, but are propagated by the fact that various university offices and units are continually engaging different community groups on a variety of projects in an unorganized, incoherent, and inconsistent fashion.

Still, many found Penn and the other area schools to be of great benefit. Even for the most marginal of residents, the university provides resources that other city institutions do not. For this reason, many were sympathetic to the university regarding criticisms about the intent and impacts of the West Philadelphia Initiatives. That sympathy, of course, came from a genuine interest in and loyalty to West Philadelphia as home. During the era of the WPI, the university's presence in West Philadelphia has a dual nature. It simultaneously presents opportunities in the form of resources and poses threats to the status quo. As one resident explained:

> It's a good resource for me. I go to the library and use the Internet there. I can go and pick through the garbage there. Stuff like that. As an institution, they're gobbling up West Philly, and it's sad because the poor just get pushed out further and further. They should be invested in building up West Philly, not reinventing it. They have so much land right now; they should be interested in taking over my building and making that college housing. I've got other places to go. It's kind of sad to see my building going unused.

Many informants complained about Penn's services for students and faculty living in West Philadelphia neighborhoods. This was particularly true of the bicycle police and the shuttle services. One of the subordinate discourses in the larger body of literature on neighborhood redevelopment and change concerns crime. Richard Taub, Garth Taylor, and Jan Dunham, in their now classic book *Paths of Neighborhood Change*, studied the relationship between residents' perceptions of crime and their psychological attachment to their neighborhood.[9] The researchers suggest that neighborhood changes are prompted by three factors: ecological conditions, corporate decisions, and individual decisions.[10] These interlocking variables contribute to neighborhood change but do not definitely cause it. A major thrust of Taub and colleagues' argument is the empirical evidence they offer that crime and racial succession patterns significantly define individual (and in some ways corporate) decision making.

In 1994, President Clinton signed the Violent Crime Control and Law Enforcement Act of 1994 (VCCA),[11] which facilitated the hiring of more than 64,000 new police officers by providing states and localities with 75 percent of the funds for new hires for three years. The objective was to stop a nationwide rise in crime that had peaked in 1991. In their analysis of the impacts of this legislation on crime rates, William Evans and Emily Owens show that, although the VCCA never met its objective of helping place a hundred thousand new officers on forces around the country, it did go a long way in helping to reduce crime.

A number of U.S. cities have experienced two years of significant increases in violent crime after a decade of historically low crime rates. Philadelphia in particular has been hard hit by this trend. In 2006, it had the highest violent crime rate among the nation's ten largest cities: 1,526 violent crimes per 100,000 residents, nearly twice the rate of Los Angeles (787) and more than twice that of New York (638).[12] Perhaps more disturbing is the fact that violent crimes in Philadelphia increased by 5.9 percent from 2005.[13] This increase was not spread evenly across the city, however. In reviewing Philadelphia's statistics for aggravated assaults between 1999 and 2005, I found that the incident rate per one thousand persons in University City had climbed by more than 60 percent, but this was still somewhat below the city's average and less than half that of some of its neighboring communities.[14]

In 2006, there was a crime spree in West Philadelphia that departed from the relative peace of the late 1990s, when the effects of the VCCA began to show. This rise in crime was perhaps because of the reversal during the early 2000s of the Clinton administration's anticrime policy. Despite some of the attention received by student muggings and attacks in the Philadelphia media outlets, crime statistics for the areas adjacent to the Penn campus are and have been kept low by the extensive and collaborative policing done by the Philadelphia Police Department, the University City District Bicycle Police (known locally as "yellow shirts"[15]), and the University of Pennsylvania Campus Police (who also ride bicycles and are known as "red shirts"). A West Philadelphia squatter shared the following with me:

> The yellow shirts—I don't like them at all. I mean, they're paid for by, like, the shadow government in West Philly. They're just like the West Philly narcs, driving around calling the police. The one last night threatened to arrest me. They don't have power of arrest. Yeah, he threatened to arrest me. I've noticed the red shirts moving further and further

out. They're out there being the gentrification police, looking out for the white kids, so they haven't messed with me. They've been nothing but nice to me when I'm trash picking on the campus. They realize that I'm not messing with the neighborhood. A lot of the red shirts I've talked to are born and raised in West Philly. The yellow shirts really aren't. The red shirts are a little more understanding. They understand the West Philly tradition of squatting a little bit more.

During the course of my research, the university installed flashing strobe lights on top of the Penn Shuttle vans that transport students and staff throughout the University City area at odd hours of the day. While the university intended the lights to make the vans more visible to waiting students, they proved to be a nuisance for area residents.

One of the strongest and most frequently aired criticisms of the university was that its dealings with area leaders, city politicians, and even different neighborhood groups were not always transparent or fair. This came up most often about the organization of the Penn-assisted elementary school. An informant explained:

Penn said that they were going to establish committees that parents could be on. They gave numbers out. It was supposed to be a wonderful demonstration school. I came home and told my constituents and neighbors that they better get on the horn, get on some of these committees and fight for your kids so some of these kids can go to that school. And I'm real sensitive to that because I was bused when I was in elementary school. I was one of the first black kids bused out of West Philadelphia, and I know that I got a better education by going to a different school. By the time the people called the next day, they were told that the committees were already established. The very next day. It was never done forthright. They were giving people lip service. They already knew what they were going to do. And it made people very angry.

According to another informant, "The only rumor I've heard [is about] their support of the shadow government of West Philly. The people who pay for the yellow shirts [security]—that they somehow pay for that or are involved in that scheme. They're just trying to eat West Philly."

While most of those interviewed knew of one or more of the university's initiatives, many did not fully understand the breadth of the WPI and were unaware of the Kromer/Kerman report that summarizes the university's activities. Sources within the university intimated that this was deliberate. Any suggestion that the initiatives were part of a larger comprehensive planning effort were to be avoided, as they might have inspired resistance from community groups or recalled the university's long history of troubled relations with West Philadelphia communities. One informant stated, "Folks as far west as Sixtieth Street are scared that Penn's going to come out there."

There was also great praise for the university and an understanding that on many levels the university was keeping West Philadelphia's interests at heart. An informant said:

Penn definitely wants the neighborhood around it to be more stable. I think that the real impetus was safety. At least while I was there. A lot of the work had started before I got there. There was a recognition that we can either build walls, or we can integrate. It was in their self-interest. Parents want to send their kids to a safe place. I actually feel like the neighborhood is [becoming] more diverse. I mean, I don't feel like it's becoming a cosmopolitan Brooklyn or Mt. Airy type [of] neighborhood. And I like that, because there aren't a lot of places in America like that.

Criticisms of the WPI for their relative lack of transparency are reminiscent of Lance Freeman's discussion of the myths of gentrification that abounded in Harlem when it went through its process of change.[16] It is simultaneously easier and more difficult to create myths about Penn's interests and agendas. The West Philadelphia Initiatives never made up a comprehensive planning document. University administrators I spoke with told me that this was intentional. Given Penn's history with Urban Renewal, a comprehensive planning document would have complicated its efforts by creating a focal point for dissenters. However, without one, residents could create myths about what the university was going to do and more weight was assigned to the WPI. Residents knew that the institution was wealthy and possessed enough political capital to get a great deal accomplished. In this case, the myths were tied to a university, which, in reality, was working on its own behalf to manage the local real estate market. The goal was to manage the many rumors about the university's intentions or plans.

A part of what created negative impressions of the university in the community was the thought that its engagement could be cyclical. Long-term residents—that is, residents who have lived in West Philadelphia for their entire lives or who belong to families who have lived there for several generations—viewed the university's engagement as being episodic. One West Philadelphia resident I spoke with belonged to a family that had lived in West Philadelphia for more than four generations and eighty years. She believed that crime rates and mortgage interest rates help determine the university's cycle of engagement. In her view, lower mortgage rates allowed investors to purchase properties that were not selling. Given other poor conditions in the area, these properties would not be profitable as single-family homes, so the investors divided them into student apartments. If crime increased, the students would look for housing in other parts of the city, yielding a housing oversupply in West Philadelphia. The overstock would cause landlords to drop rents and fill their apartments with renters with few other options. Through their neglect of neighborhood social mores and standards, renters would invite other elements and residents to view these communities as blighted and in decline.

The vicious cycle would continue until the university intervened with public safety initiatives or other efforts aimed at making the area more attractive to university faculty, staff, and students, or until market conditions made the sale of single-family homes attractive for investors and home buyers.

Despite Penn's reported success, tensions remain. At the close of the West Philadelphia Initiatives and the transfer of university leadership from Rodin to Gutmann, many community leaders used Gutmann's inaugural as an opportunity to express displeasure about how West Philadelphia had changed during the Rodin years. The critique was that Penn had prospered and that the residents of West Philadelphia had not. Anecdotal evidence of rising rents and property values permeated the discourse about neighborhood change and became manifest in posters, community newsletters, and other local news reporting that challenged the university to increase its social and economic inclusion activities and work to mitigate the effects of its policies on the poorest segments of the surrounding neighborhoods.

For the most part, this chapter and its data exist primarily because various informants suggested other explanations for neighborhood change in West Philadelphia. Naturally, many of these are obvious, but given the university's assumption of successes in urban revitalization, it seems best to place those successes (and failures) in their proper context. Many of the alternative explanations discussed in this chapter deserve their own rigorous analysis. Their inclusion is intended to describe a few of the many other redevelopment efforts that took place, or are currently taking place, alongside Penn's. The extent to which these competing variables have contributed to the overall patterns of urban change in West Philadelphia are unclear. I identified the themes and initiatives of demographic shifts, regional economic restructuring, national-level crime trends, and "other" redevelopment projects as being the most frequently mentioned in the interviews.

Aside from the factors already mentioned that changed the composition and character of West Philadelphia, many informants noted the significance of the area's aging population. A survey of census data at the tract level between 1990 and 2009 does not show dramatic changes in neighborhood composition in this area.[17] Between 2000 and 2009, the median age for the University City area remained a consistent 25.3 years. This is not to suggest that there have not been some changes. Some tracts experienced wide swings in their median ages, with many becoming much younger presumably as students moved into areas that were not options for them before the WPI. The movement of families and professionals into other parts of University City increased the median ages in those areas, providing a stable median age. There was a small change (a 2 percent increase) in the percentage of University City residents with graduate and professional degrees between 1990 and 2009 and a drop (three percentage points to 7.3 percent) in the unemployment rate for the population over sixteen years of age.

Despite the $5.5 million and nearly 800 mortgages provided to Penn faculty and staff in University City, the proportion of owners to renters has remained relatively unchanged. The reasons for this are perhaps multiple, and resident informants are a useful source of information for perspective on this phenomenon. As buildings were upgraded by the university through the Fund, other property owners also moved to renovate their properties and raise rents to capture the student housing market. Simultaneously, a process of invasion and neighborhood succession may have been occurring, leaving the proportions of renters to homesteading property owners virtually intact.

Several data points reveal how these changes are reflected on the ground. The first is the relative proportion of racial groups. The percentage of white residents in University City tracts started at 47.4 percent in 1990, dropped to 38.4 percent in 2000, and rebounded to 48.2 percent in 2009. The black population remained steady between 1990 and 2000 at 42 percent and then dropped to 32 percent in 2009. There was also an increase in the Asian population. Another important data point that reflects how things have changed in West Philadelphia is housing affordability. Common standards of affordability suggest that households should not spend more than 30 percent of their income on housing costs. Between 1990 and 2009, the average percentage of income spent on housing in West Philadelphia went from a barely affordable 29 percent to 34 percent. Had the recession not stagnated housing sales and prices in University City starting in 2008, that number might have been higher.

Other Revitalization/Development Initiatives

Many of the participants in this study continually pointed to other factors that were contributing to the neighborhood changes they were experiencing. Economic restructuring is perhaps the single most significant direct or indirect feature of large-scale changes in Philadelphia's neighborhoods. It does not go without saying that many of the initiatives outlined below, and many features of the WPI, focus on place-based improvements or enhancements to institutions and structures that have been affected by economic restructuring. The policy implications of this for low-income communities can be extrapolated from Sugrue's analysis of Detroit. As in that city, in Philadelphia African American workers fought hard to gain access to unionized manufacturing jobs at the precise moment when these jobs began to evaporate.[18] While professional and technical occupations have replaced a fraction of the manufacturing jobs lost, they are often offered only to workers with college degrees.

The new economic outlook for low-skilled workers in Philadelphia involves access to service jobs in the sprawling, and transit-deficient, suburbs and low-paying retail and clerical jobs in the urban center. The city's colleges and universities—especially Penn—provide the lion's share of those jobs. That the occupational status of West Philadelphia residents in particular has changed dramatically over the past fifty years is in large part because of the effects of deindustrialization. West Philadelphia, one of the older parts of the city, has been particularly hard hit by this process. Its northern and southern ends were at one time linked to light manufacturing industries. Between 1990 and 2000, University City lost nearly 4,100 manufacturing jobs.

The collective workforces of the University of Pennsylvania, Drexel, the University of the Sciences, area hospitals, and the Science Center account for nearly 35,000 jobs.[19] A job cluster of that size not only rivals the central business district; it also represents one of the largest in the Commonwealth of Pennsylvania. The University of Pennsylvania alone (without the Medical Center) can boast that it is the Commonwealth's second largest private employer and

Philadelphia's largest by a wide margin.[20] The degree to which that employment base is rooted in West Philadelphia remains to be understood. Based on the commuting patterns of West Philadelphians, it is a safe assumption that a majority are within walking distance of their workplaces.

Qualitative data from interviews suggest that access to that job market appears to be as elusive for low-skilled, noncollege-educated West Philadelphians as is admission to its undergraduate colleges. Labor force participation rates indicate that disparities remain between whites and African Americans, as they do in per capita and household incomes. Rising housing prices may further skew this pattern in years to come as lower-income African Americans flee to outlying areas and inner-ring suburbs in search of affordable housing.

Numerous other efforts initiated by federal, state, and local government have had impacts on patterns of change not just in University City but in Philadelphia as a whole. The following discussion of these efforts should not be taken as a comprehensive treatment or as a comparison of their impacts with those of the university's revitalization efforts. Instead, they should be interpreted as playing a role—however large or small—in the broadest possible conceptions of change. What is important about them is their geographical location within the orbit of Penn's work. Only in the cases of the city's Neighborhood Transformation Initiative and its rapid transit line refurbishment do these projects intersect with the West Philadelphia community.

In 1994, the Philadelphia Empowerment Zone was established by the Clinton administration, via the Department of Housing and Urban Development, to aid redevelopment of the city's most distressed areas through a mix of tax incentives and social services. This was a national program designed to reverse the deleterious urban policy of the previous twelve years of the Reagan and Bush administrations and, specifically, Reagan's "enterprise zone" program.[21]

Locally, city leaders, such as former mayor and now Pennsylvania governor Edward Rendell and current Mayor John Street, saw the Empowerment Zone program as a way to make good on promises they had made earlier to turn the focus toward neighborhoods after so much political and economic capital investment in Center City.[22] The program merits attention here not only because it appears to have been successful in Philadelphia but also because one of the key empowerment zones abuts University City (the western edge of West Powelton and the northern edge of Walnut Hill/ Garden Court). The revival of the street car along Girard Avenue in 2004 and the relative successes of the Girard Avenue Coalition in developing that commercial corridor and some of the residential neighborhoods that align with it were possibly aided by a combined West Philadelphia/Center City spillover effect.[23]

In 2001, Philadelphia Mayor John Street launched an ambitious effort to address decades of decline in Philadelphia neighborhoods, known as the Neighborhood Transformation Initiative (NTI).[24] With a total project budget of $295 million, the campaign focused on two key strategies: land assembly and blight eradication in areas where the city's efforts might best inspire private investment. Practically, this meant that the city would acquire and bulldoze abandoned properties and then redevelop them. Mayor Street used the NTI as an opportunity to realign some city departments and direct them to work in a more integrated fashion to support NTI's success. A key and very visible example of this was the coordination of several city offices to increase the volume of abandoned cars removed from neighborhood streets.

In many ways, this work facilitated the construction of new low-rise housing developments that required more land than did the high-rise or denser public housing that was dismantled with the aid of HOPE VI funds. Two studies of NTI have been published. The first, Philadelphia's *The Reinvestment Fund*, was engaged early with NTI in a market value analysis (MVA) to guide the city's efforts. The result was a six-tiered typology that characterized areas as "regional choice," "high value," "steady," "transitional," "stressed," "reclamation," and "non-residential."[25] The second study on NTI, a doctoral thesis by Lisa Bates, analyzed its spillover effects. Bates concluded that a range of other factors contributed to redevelopment and property valorization in many parts of the city after the start of the NTI program.

NTI is important for an analysis of Penn's work in Philadelphia, which geographically overlapped with NTI in a number of places around University City. In my interviews with residents from each of the major University City neighborhoods, I most often encountered "NTI spillover" in the Walnut Hill neighborhood, where a great deal of effort had been invested on the blocks of Sansom and Chestnut Streets between Fortieth and Forty-Sixth Streets. Residents of this twelve-block area successfully prevented Penn from acquiring the property for a nursing home, and prevented the city from acquiring it for a homeless shelter. The continued construction along their street because of NTI, as well as a new set of social relations emerging from the influxes of new residents who were mostly Penn staff taking advantage of the Penn's mortgage programs, created a "hot spot" of renewal in a very troubled section of the neighborhood.

Stephen McGovern, who wrote one of the only comprehensive evaluations of NTI, concludes that the effort was ambitious and had great potential to deal with the city's stock of blighted and abandoned properties.[26] Yet, he says, despite high hopes for success in both Philadelphia and in national-level urban policy circles, the effort lagged and did not achieve as much as it might have had the mayor's interest and support been sustained over time. The relative lack of engagement by community development corporations and the focus on leveraging private capital for housing construction took the NTI's focus off affordable housing and put it on housing for middle-class and upper-middle-class families. In the University City/West Philadelphia context, NTI performed the tasks Penn-driven and community-based efforts could not or would not carry out, such as removing abandoned cars and reclaiming vacant lots.

Another significant improvement project that contributed to West Philadelphia's rebirth was the renovation of the Southeastern Pennsylvania Transportation Authority's (SEPTA) Market-Frankford elevated subway. Constructed by the Philadelphia Rapid Transit Company and operational since 1907, this is the city's oldest rapid transit line.[27] Two key components of the rehabilitation project may prove critical to the viability of West Philadelphia small businesses. Many of the current stations along the Market-Frankford elevated are situated at the top of the intersection of two arterial streets (Market Street being the one they all share). Almost by default, each intersection has come to serve as bus depot, public commons, and retail corridor. By eliminating half of the columns that support the line's tracks, project architects hope to invigorate these intersections by enhancing pedestrian and vehicle traffic flow. Each station is being completely rebuilt to include modern conveniences such as elevators, wheelchair access, and improved lighting in and underneath.

Summary

The view that community groups were assisted by the University of Pennsylvania in their attempts to redevelop and "save" their communities is correct but somewhat flawed. Penn's view of its role overstates its importance in reversing urban decline. West Philadelphia neighborhoods experienced a precipitous drop in crime that was driven by Penn, the University City District, the Philadelphia Police Department, and community public safety organizations. However, those efforts took place at a time when crime rates and urban crime rates in particular were dropping nationally.

The same can be said for housing values and their appreciation. The real estate boom of the late 1990s and early 2000s spurred radical housing price gains in many metropolitan-area markets. A cursory analysis of comparative housing appreciation rates reveals that Philadelphia's rates lagged behind those of other northeastern cities during the same period. The most stable and attractive residential areas of Philadelphia thus became fertile ground for real estate speculators in search of unexploited markets. Also attractive to speculators was Philadelphia's relative proximity to the unaffordable housing markets of Washington and New York and its relative affordability. Then historically low interest rates nationwide only spurred this speculation in real estate.

Penn's investment in the University City neighborhoods, which are incidentally those closest to the tight housing market of Philadelphia's central business district, also hastened speculation in these areas. In this scenario, Penn served as the promoter, not the master engineer. Improvements to retail and public education accentuated this process. In a local context, such improvements may appear to have been the key to neighborhood revitalization, but instead they may only have been a significant, but micro-level, factor in the transformation of West Philadelphia. Penn could not and cannot control or influence national trends in crime, interest rates, housing market appreciation, and the like, but it could and can benefit from them locally by understanding the trends and leveraging its own policy to maximize their impacts on its host communities. At some point, home values do come to reflect appraisal prices in that they can create wealth for sellers. That wealth bears implications for the standard of living sellers are able to afford after a sale.

In Chapter 4, I explore the contemporary dual nature of urban revitalization. This is an appropriate chapter to follow the discussion here of what I learned from West Philadelphia residents. There is no single, easy answer to the question of whether the University of Pennsylvania has made significant improvements to the quality of life in its local context. As the preceding pages show, there have been real improvements in educational options and retail and housing quality. There have also been clear reductions in crime and spending by the university with local entrepreneurs. At the same time, it is clear that there was a context to those successes and that similar efforts to stabilize or improve the area's housing stock might have been more difficult or impossible after the start of the Great Recession. Crime rates may drop for a time but rise again without vigilance, continued investment, and a clear understanding of how area crime may be related to larger trends in the city and region. In other words, improvements may be ephemeral without a larger commitment by the university.

If nothing else, this chapter reveals that West Philadelphians are viewing the results of the WPI as mixed. The university led a revitalization program that encompassed both place-based (housing, retail, beautification) and people-based (crime reduction, schools, local spending) approaches. It is important to note that the two approaches are not mutually exclusive. For example, the Penn-Alexander School simultaneously represents a service, an investment in human capital, a strategy to improve investments in the area's real estate, an employer, and a community resource center. These types of improvements were welcomed; however, the unintended consequences and impacts are only partially documented here and well beyond the view of the casual observer.

4

The Dual Nature of Revitalization in the Twenty-First Century

Media coverage of the West Philadelphia story speaks of rapid and positive revitalization. This chapter presents evidence that speaks of the emerging dual nature of current urban revitalization, the contemporary measure of which has taken a decided turn away from poverty alleviation and incumbent upgrading toward more place-based solutions. Here I suggest that this shift is particularly problematic when left to the well-intentioned planning interests and activities of private institutions such as colleges and universities.

This chapter also suggests that the impacts of the University of Pennsylvania's revitalization efforts can be analyzed only with an understanding of how the university's role in this particular case of neighborhood change is related to a broad and diffuse literature. I present here an analysis of other studies of neighborhood change that reveal how conceptions of change and revitalization are inherently subjective and political.[1] Conflicts over the conceptualization of the term *revitalization* lead various constituencies to engage in contests to control public space, schools, public safety agendas, and other urban quality-of-life issues. The studies chosen for review discuss how these conflicts reflect the political economy of American cities and society. Conceptions of crime prevention, housing rehabilitation, and improved public education are influenced by racial and class tensions, and are ultimately shaped by white middle-class ethnocentrism. Stated differently, the term *revitalization* mischaracterizes working-class and poor neighborhoods by defining them as socially disorganized places.[2] The reinvasion of these areas by middle-class residents (and in this case university students, faculty, and staff) in the 1970s through the 1990s was organized around the tastes of incoming groups and not around the material and social reality of those communities.

My brief thematic synopsis of three ethnographic studies of urban neighborhood change—Elijah Anderson's *Streetwise*, Brett Williams's *Upscaling Downtown*, and William Julius Wilson and Richard Taub's *There Goes the Neighborhood*—is followed by a discussion of how the themes I highlight connect to broader contemporary analyses of neighborhood change and revitalization.[3] Both concepts are nested within larger sociological and planning literatures.

The area of research now dominating the revitalization discourse is gentrification, a phenomenon that has captured the attention of progressive academics who are concerned about the role it may play in the displacement of incumbent low-income populations from the inner city. Gentrification has also captured the attention of neoliberal policy makers who suggest that it may simultaneously inspire broad private reinvestment at the urban core and in disperse pockets of concentrated poverty.

The next section is a brief discussion of two narratives of urban change in which universities made significant contributions. These studies look at the role that the University of Chicago and the University of Pennsylvania played in containing the race-based neighborhood succession that "threatened" to place their campuses in the center of predominantly African American neighborhoods.

The chapter concludes with the suggestion that the literature of contemporary planning and sociology is lacking in narratives of the contributions of universities to urban redevelopment and revitalization in the post–Cold War, postindustrial, knowledge-centered urban economy.

In the United States, the notion of neighborhood change can mean many things, but primarily it involves neighborhood decline and/or revitalization. I employ a broad definition that refers to revitalization and more specifically to the upgrading or improvement of previously blighted or decrepit urban conditions.[4] Such a definition encompasses several relevant topics, including gentrification. However, while it is sufficient in a general way, new modes of inner city revitalization have attempted to settle the debate by creating new definitions that center on real estate development, quality of life, and profit generation as metrics of success or effectiveness.[5]

In the course of the research and in subsequent chapters, I used the broader term *neighborhood change* so that both my own and my informants' perspectives would not be informed by normative ideas of urban neighborhood revitalization. This is largely because of the variation and politicization of the terms *revitalization* and, to a greater extent, *gentrification* in academic discourse. For this reason, I focus on how residents conceptualize and interpret the changes in their neighborhoods. In many ways, the perception of change, social cohesion, and conflict in evolving urban neighborhoods better reflects reality than do objective measures of improved quality of life.

Narratives of Urban Neighborhood Change

An examination of the social science literature reveals many approaches to the study of urban neighborhood change. I have identified three narratives that are relevant to this study—Elijah Anderson's *Streetwise*, Brett Williams's *Upscaling Downtown*, and William Julius Wilson and Richard Taub's *There Goes the Neighborhood*. Each engages issues of gentrification and racial change in areas being upgraded and "revitalized."[6] Moreover, each deals with the question of whether gentrification/revitalization (or the lack of it) facilitates the entry of new groups and alters neighborhood social structures. In addition, all ask how those altered social relations impair the quality of life for economically disadvantaged or marginalized groups.

While each study deals with a set of issues unique to its study area, race and class tensions are common to all three. In some way, each discusses intra- and intergroup relations (e.g., African American and white; old and young; homeowner and renter; middle class and poor) that shape the contestation over urban space and judgments about the degree and value of neighborhood change. With varying success, each also addresses (implicitly or explicitly) agency and victimization. What follows is a synopsis of the themes found in these narratives as well as suggestions for how they are linked to the case of Penn/University City, West Philadelphia.

Crime

Crime pervades the social science literature as a key issue in neighborhood change and revitalization.[7] As with many other issues, perceptions of crime are not always consistent with actual measures of it.[8] Naturally, perceptions of crime in the broader literature and in the three studies here are obfuscated by preconceived notions about its sources—teenagers, African Americans, the poor. In Anderson's "Northton," Williams's "Elm Valley," and Wilson and Taub's Chicago (the communities studied by the ethnographies), crime prevention and/or reduction were a central part of the narrative of change. Either the area became more attractive because popular perceptions of its crime were improving or revitalization made crime reduction a central part of the process.

Perceptions of crime are almost as important as actual experiences with it in how they feed intra- and intergroup conflicts. Older homeowners blamed teenagers for area crime while incoming young professionals possessed only tenuous social relations with members of different ethnic groups for fear of being victimized. This is particularly clear in Williams's *Upscaling Downtown*, where housing choices and daily behavior were governed by fear of the drug trade. What Williams adds to this discussion that the others do not is how perceptions are sometimes bolstered by information that is not tied to local events. The perceptions of many of Williams's "Elm Valley" residents were colored not only by race and age but also by representations of their community and city on television and popular media. In *Streetwise*, Anderson depicts another feature of crime. As the other two studies found, he discovered that the growing drug trade diminished a collective sense of safety among area residents that affected their ability to socialize with cross-identity thresholds (homeowner and renter, young and old, African American and white).

Intra- and Intergroup Conflict

One of the most common misconceptions in the study of neighborhood change is that all conflict involves neighborhood identity, especially between newcomers and long-time residents. On many levels, this has been a common feature of neighborhood revitalization in U.S. cities since 1970, but various other tensions are created and exposed through the revitalization process, and intra-group conflict among African Americans is one of them. Based largely on class and resident status (renter versus home owner), many home-owning African Americans attempt to control social relations and neighborhood conditions by managing social mores. In *Streetwise*, Anderson discusses the various ways in which African American middle-class homeowners attempted to distance themselves from African American renters. They distanced themselves from youth and men in particular—for example, by changing their manner of speaking and claiming to have never lived in the ghetto. This distancing was on one level the same fear-based response that matched other residents' responses to crime. In many ways, it extended to the ways middle-class African Americans attempted to "manage" the behavior of the poor and, by extension, the identity of Williams's Northton as a desirable place to live.

Wilson and Taub speak to a similar issue in their analysis of the "Groveland" area of Chicago. For Groveland's middle-class African American residents, neighborhood preservation was important for containing the poverty and blight that was encroaching on their long-standing, respectable, and stable community.

All three studies found that tensions existed most often between homeowners and renters. For new and somewhat more transient middle–class professionals who were only connected to their homes as investments and not for social ties, the tension was somewhat muted. For long-term residents, the perceived and actual crime and nuisances they experienced were often associated with poor and transient renters who lacked significant concerns for the quality of life in their home community.

Agency and Victimization

A central question in the debate over revitalization/gentrification is whether the process necessarily involves displacement of the poor. Some scholarship suggests that displacement is not a default out-come of neighborhood change.[9] Some neighborhood improve-ments may actually benefit residents and encourage them to remain in their homes and neighborhoods. Some changes may have nega-tive impacts, but they may also have positive ones. Furthermore, one reason to review the studies here is to demonstrate that notions of community development fail to recognize how social institutions impact processes of change.

Increased housing costs, associated with higher property values and assessments, may contribute to displacement more directly than does violent eviction from rental properties. What Anderson, Williams, and Wilson and Taub contribute to this discussion is evidence that so-cial networks and resources that once supported vulnerable constitu-ent groups are diminished by the circumstances of change.

Williams's study is particularly useful for showing how, even with stalled or slow gentrification, social networks can be adversely af-fected in short periods. Although Williams's analysis discusses a case where regional economic trends stalled gentrification in Washington, D.C., the influx of young white urban professionals still had a sig-nificant impact. New residents did not engage with established social mores such as food sharing, and shared responsibility for street clean-ing and youth discipline diminished in importance. Scholars such as Carol Stack (*All Our Kin*) and Katherine Newman (*No Shame in My Game*) have shown how the poor, and poor women of color in particular, depend on social networks to survive.[10] The disruption of these networks has real economic consequences for the poor and should not be dismissed as mere sentimentality and nostalgia.

Schools

After crime, a lack of faith in urban school systems looms large as a factor that drives home-buying decisions. Planning literature on schools and community development shows that middle-class residents choose their homes based more on school quality and choice than on other factors.[11] The studies here reveal that public education is in many ways a central feature of vibrant and cohesive communities, but it is also a controversial amenity that can inspire in- or out-migration.

Wilson and Taub's treatment of the subject stands out as they highlight the degree to which racial segregation is contingent on the view that particular schools are "bad" based on the proportion of African American students they enroll. Sadly, this view is not unique to white-dominated areas, but is common in Latino-dominated areas as well. In their study, Wilson and Taub describe a coalition of parents that challenged the catchments area definitions of their neighborhood schools so that African American students would not be bused in and particular communities would have exclusive access to a well-regarded magnet school located in a predominantly African American neighborhood.

In all three studies, crime, schools, intergroup conflict (or social cohesiveness), and race emerge as areas where neighbors exhibit similar responses to wildly different phenomena. But, as Wilson and Taub show, the integration of churches, civic organizations (e.g., Rotary Club), or retail amenities does not involve the same long-term and daily commitments that school enrollment does. As an amenity, school quality—as interpreted by the racial composition of community schools—is an embodiment of class status and tensions.

Urban Neighborhood Change: A Review

In this section I demonstrate how the ethnographies of Williams, Wilson and Taub, and Anderson, and the one to be discussed in this section, fit with the diffuse and undertheorized literature on urban neighborhood change. Interdisciplinary literature on this subject contains a wealth of empirical evidence on processes and outcomes but offers weak theoretical frameworks with which to examine alternative variables and factors. What follows is a discussion of dominant and contemporary studies and explanations of change from the fields of sociology, anthropology, planning, and public policy.

A necessary preliminary is defining the term *neighborhood*. Urban neighborhoods have long served as basic units of social analysis because of the extent to which they reflect residents' social structures and dynamics based on proximity, shared identities, interests, and histories. They can alternatively be understood through their physical and social characteristics.[12] As with larger spatial units such as cities, counties, or states, geographic features or a unique population distinguish one neighborhood from another. Unlike larger spatial units, however, neighborhoods often have a system of rules, norms, and regularly recurring patterns of social interaction that serve to control social behavior; they also have unique patterns of social behavior.[13]

The term *neighborhood* has been challenged in recent years to reflect the "placelessness" of neighborhoods today.[14] Such definitions fail to appreciate the porous nature of neighborhoods, their social networks, and structures. While natural barriers may limit a neighborhood's spatial coverage, they may not limit much else. More contemporary definitions of *neighborhood* recognize that individuals and families may remain socially connected to inner-city neighborhoods and their institutions despite having emigrated to the suburbs.[15] Thus, according to Harvey, neighborhoods are not communities, and communities are not neighborhoods.[16]

The study of urban neighborhood change can be roughly divided into five theoretical frameworks: (1) demographic-ecological, (2) sociocultural (3) political-economic (4) community network, and (5) social network.[17] A massive volume of scholarly writing attempts to explain urban change through one or more of these. While a great deal of this work is best understood as sociological, many planners and other social scientists have also contributed to it. I discuss two frameworks here: demographic-ecological and political-economic.

Chronologically, the older and most established of the theoretical frameworks is demographic-ecological, which includes the
invasion-succession and urban life cycle schools of thought. These
schools were founded by Roderick McKenzie and E. M. Hoover
and R. Vernon, respectively.[18] Demographic-ecological themes center on assumptions that different social groups (populations) engage
in competition, conflict, and accommodation regarding urban space.
In the United States in particular, the phenomenon of race compli-
cates the simple ecological metaphor Robert E. Park writes about
in *The City* (1925), and it has led later generations of social scientists
to develop more complex theories of change that considered racial
and status transitions.[19] For the second half of the twentieth century,
urban sociologists were consumed with the "tipping point"—that is,
the quantitative measure of the threshold at which whites cede their
neighborhoods to nonwhites. Subsequent research showed that the
path of change in urban neighborhoods is too variable to strictly follow either Park's model or the tipping point hypothesis; however, as
a matter of planning and policy, patterns of racial succession in urban
neighborhoods were also connected to economic considerations.

Similarly, the life cycle hypothesis of neighborhood change presumed that urban neighborhoods would experience stages that included a number of cycles of invasion-succession or, more generally,
growth and decline. Given its roots in the demographic-ecological
framework, this hypothesis also presupposed many things about the
settlement patterns of people of color. One of the most important
and central themes in discussions of inner-city poverty for more
than sixty years has been race.

This theme of race in urban poverty may be even older, dat-
ing back to W.E.B. DuBois's publication of *The Philadelphia Negro*
in 1899 by the University of Pennsylvania Press. Commissioned by
the socially progressive heiress Susan P. Wharton and University of
Pennsylvania provost Charles C. Harrison, this study was intended
to understand "why blacks in Philadelphia were not participating in
the society at levels that would give them a decent standard of living
and enable them to make positive contributions to the political and
social world of the city."[20] DuBois instead set out to enlighten his

sponsors and other Philadelphia elites about the fortunes of African Americans in the city at that time. DuBois's biographer Davis Lewis suggests that DuBois's sponsors' different view of his commission was tainted by their desire to sequester the perceived social disorganization and pestilence of the city's growing African American and immigrant communities.[21]

During his data collection, DuBois's view of the project and his own hypothesis changed. He was not simply conducting a census of Philadelphia's seventh ward but attempting to explain a complex system of discrimination and exclusion in the Philadelphia labor market that had had a destabilizing effect on individual workers, families, and the community at large. The ideological perspectives and the policy informed by *The Philadelphia Negro* that blamed the poor for their economic circumstances were in many ways implicitly race based. The divide that existed between liberals and conservatives who debated the extent to which structural factors, economic restructuring, widespread institutional and legally sanctioned racism, and spatial segregation of metropolitan regions was more to blame than aggregated individual characteristics. These debates are as present in our current politics as they were fifty years ago, when President Lyndon B. Johnson launched his War on Poverty.

Over time, structural explanations also defined as political-economic came to challenge the dominance of the demographic-ecological and life cycle frameworks. Two examples are Susan S. Fainstein and Norman Fainstein's "urban structuration" and David Harvey's "spatial fix."[22] With the (partial) shift from ecological to structural explanations, the examination of the intersection of race and class—or, more explicitly, the link between race and poverty—came to dominate the study of urban neighborhoods in the 1980s and early 1990s.

For more than fifty years, planners and policy makers have been on a quest to know how best to deal with the problems of the American inner city.[23] In my assessment, there is a divide between studies of urban change that seek to understand the concept as a phenomenon and those that view it as a process. The debates about definitions of neighborhood revitalization are both diachronic and dialogic. Most can agree that revitalization involves an improvement of conditions; few, however, can agree on the mode or metrics of improvement. In academic and community activist circles, urban revitalization is seen as incorporating social and economic justice and equity. For practicing planners and developers, on the other hand, revitalization has come to mean real estate development, as evidenced by quality of life issues such as housing and its associated amenities (e.g., retail, transportation access, schools).

An appreciation for the longer history of American urban life reveals that urban decline is the result of a combination of economic reorganization of metropolitan and global markets and, in the case of racial and ethnic minorities, racism.[24] Thus, the story of American cities for the better part of the twentieth century involved the pernicious effects of this calamitous recipe.

Despite nearly a century of scholarship and policy, cities and their troubled inner neighborhoods are still not well understood to be a reflection of the structural forces that shape them. For many, they are popularly viewed as "symbols of the failure of an activist government and well-intentioned, but naïve liberalism."[25] For over twenty years, the academic literature on the causes and effects of and potential solutions to the intersection of race and poverty in American cities has been largely shaped by two interconnected ideological divides. Liberal scholars such as William Julius Wilson and Douglas Massey have debated for two decades whether "race" or "space" plays a more dominant role in defining the life chances of inner-city African Americans. Wilson argued in his book, *The Truly Disadvantaged*, that inner-city poverty was becoming more pronounced and concentrated as middle-class African-Americans retreated from central cities, leaving behind the poorest and most socially marginal. Douglas S. Massey and Nancy A. Denton skillfully argued in response that, while poverty was becoming more concentrated and severe, the true source of the spatial "pulling apart" was to be found in white racism.[26]

Both camps agreed somewhat on the structural sources of inner-city poverty. In contrast, conservative writers have focused not on these structural sources but on individual character traits and failings.

Further, the "personal failings" of the poor were compounded by misguided government policy that enabled them to be perpetuated. With the inauguration of Ronald Reagan, government policy at the federal level began reversing nearly forty years of New Deal policies even though the effects of emerging global capitalism could be felt by low-skill, low-wage American workers. By extension, just as in DuBois's time, predominantly African American neighborhoods reflected the disconnection of working-age adults to local labor markets.

In this analysis, I seek to demonstrate that definitions of revitalization must contain elements of a structural view of poverty and the dynamics of race and class. In my belief, the ongoing debates in academic/policy circles on the causes of and solutions to poverty misguide and misinform public policy making. Second, I seek to support the well-established thesis that the neglect or dismissal of structural analyses of poverty in public policy making has spatial implications for cities and regions.[27] Where neighborhood improvement based on the liberal/structural analysis tends to focus on incumbent upgrading and improving the quality of life in urban areas, revitalization that focuses only on the latter supports policy that avoids human development in favor of place development.

Just as with *revitalization*, there is considerable disagreement about the definition of *gentrification*. Also, like the revitalization debate, the debate over gentrification has grown somewhat diachronic as research on the causes and effects of gentrification have improved. Marxist geographers have long argued that patterns of capital investment and disinvestment are tied to investment cycles and geography.[28] Proximity to the city center creates a pattern of investment that favors areas closest to it.[29] Neil Smith, John J. Palen, and Bruce London have shaped the discourse on gentrification to focus on the presupposition of displacement and the continued marginalization of low-income communities and people of color.[30] More contemporary writers such as Loretta Lees, Elvin Wyly, and Tom Slater have pushed the discourse further by challenging the literature to consider alternative perspectives.[31] As with *revitalization*, various definitions of *gentrification* exist, although these appear to be more evenly divided between market and social forces.

Critiques of the Marxist/structural school of thought suggest that economic arguments are not sufficient to explain all of the change that gentrification creates. Gentrification (and to some extent revitalization) is an ideology, and as such it places great importance on the role of individuals in private investment decisions and their ability to make rational economic choices about housing and amenities. Because gentrification, as a term, is saddled with this baggage, it has become an invidious word that developers and individual homebuyers seek to avoid. This is partly because of the implicit assumptions about the victimization of low-income communities and people of color. However, it appears to be advantageous to remain in gentrifying areas as services and amenities improve.

I suggest that the debate over the potential advantages to gentrification reflects what Tom Slater terms "the eviction of critical perspectives."[32] The relative increase in the number of "soft" critiques of gentrification and its impacts and the failure to appreciate how those have evolved over the past thirty years obscure the larger view of it. In his book, *The Neoliberal City*, Jason Hackworth presents evidence from New York showing that gentrification has evolved beyond the domain of small private pioneers to being something that only "corporate gentrifiers"—developers with enough capital to invest in valorized inner-city markets—can engage in.[33] Thus, the view that gentrification is simply a contest of values between low-income and middle-class or wealthy residents is incorrect and outdated. The discourse must be updated to reflect the new reality of urban investment and development.

This book recognizes the ongoing debate about the planning's field's "mission" and focus. In the introduction to the second edition of their seminal planning theory text, Fainstein and Campbell characterize planning as operating on three planes.[34] The first is to serve as a corrective for the failures of the market (Klosterman).[35] The second is to constantly and consistently confront and challenge the market to plan in the public interest (Harvey, Smith).[36] The third is to assist the market in doing what it does—expand itself and its profits for capital (Friedan and Sagalyn).[37] Narratives of what was lost in the redevelopment of Times Square are, in Lynn Sagalyn's assessment, "nostalgia" and an anti-intellectual, uncritical view of the larger process and its impacts. This relates to the previous discussion of the divisions among sociologists on the causes of social dislocations in inner-city communities and the eviction from the discourse of critical perspectives on gentrification.

It may be difficult to locate an ideological shift within the planning field from progressive to neoliberal. However, the declining prominence of subfields of planning such as community development and of topics such as equity and advocacy planning speaks to, at the very least, a thematic shift away from social concerns. In the void thus created, urban communities are left to their own devices or must rely on the assistance of private developers, community development corporations, and municipal-level urban policy.

Narratives of University-Led Urban Revitalization and Change

Given the failure of planners and other social scientists to define *revitalization*, few studies adequately assess the relationship between specific institutions and urban revitalization and change.[38] As I argue in Chapter 6, the relationship between cities and higher education has grown more complex with time. The reality is that universities in the United States have a long history of attempting urban revitalization. However, the modes of that revitalization have varied over time.

In previous attempts at revitalization, goals often involved a focus on limiting racial succession in neighborhoods close to campus.[39] Universities also attempted to recreate their urban contexts to suit new purposes. The narratives of these attempts are primarily historical studies that provide extraordinary detail about institutional and community decision making and responses to change, but they lack a "crucial level of experience" that ethnography provides.[40] Both Arnold Hirsch and Margaret O'Mara review the experience of the universities of Chicago and Pennsylvania in the 1940s–1960s and the 1950s–1960s, respectively, when racial succession and neighborhood transition were colluding with rapid deindustrialization to create the urban crisis. Neither Chicago nor Philadelphia is today the dire and dark place they describe.[41]

Overall, the studies that are the focus of this chapter—Anderson, Williams, and Wilson and Taub—fail to consider the extent to which the regional and global restructuring of the economy may have affected the neighborhoods themselves. I contend that detailed understanding of local institutions and the impacts economic restructuring had on them—and how they responded to those impacts—are critical pieces of the puzzle. Moreover, these studies fail to provide a sense of place (Wilson and Taub more so than Anderson) that would provide critical details about social relations and structures as they operate and exist in situ.

In summary, while there is nothing new in the debate about the political nature of planning, revitalization needs to be understood as one of many planning concepts that are based on normative assumptions of what cities should be.[42] As I discuss in Chapter 5, universities are evolving to meet the challenges of the twentieth-first century and coming to be critically assessed as dominant capital actors in their local contexts. Therefore, it is now necessary to distill the evolved definition of *revitalization*, which has gone from its historical dual meaning (spatial mobility versus incumbent upgrading) to the layered nonnormative meaning it now possesses.

To appreciate fully the complexity of the influence a fiscally resource-rich research university might have on patterns of change, housing patterns, and social structures, we must consider the meta-level effects of its presence and engagement. While it is constructive to measure the university's impact on the housing and labor markets, the creation and enhancement of the local retail and commercial corridors, and so on, it is also useful to connect those measurements to larger theoretical frameworks of the knowledge region and social exclusion.

In current times, the analysis of the roles universities may play in urban neighborhood change and revitalization, and the impacts of those roles, is complicated by the ascendance of the knowledge economy. The literature on the knowledge economy, particularly the learning region literature, places high importance on privileging the skilled and highly educated (to the explicit detriment of the un-skilled).[43] Manuel Castells offers a solution:

> The key to fighting self-reproducing marginality is access both to jobs and to income generation. For this, *education* is a must: general education, not narrow job training. Rather it is the transformation of the residents of these communities, by finding jobs and earning income outside the community that will change their character.[44]

The character change that Castells writes about has, in some senses, come about in West Philadelphia and elsewhere. It is clear that we are seeing a change in the concentration of poverty in many metropolitan regions versus a significant decrease in the total proportion of all persons living in poverty. The emergence of the knowledge industry, and its agglomeration on an island of innovation and industry with a research university as its core, only serves to deepen the chasm between undereducated and low-skilled workers and the labor force. What distinguishes this chasm from the geographic nature of traditional spatial mismatch theory is that many of these workers currently live or once lived adjacent to these growing job centers.

The physical manifestation of this duality has consequences for low-income or marginalized communities in how services and amenities are geared toward knowledge workers. In economic terms, this is manifest in the decreasing affordability of everything from groceries to entertainment and, more important, housing. The duality may seem more apparent in "global cities," where the dependence on "financial and corporate sectors dominate[s] redevelopment agendas."[45]

5

Comparative Views of Contemporary University-Driven Neighborhood Change

espite the economic downturn, many universities are working to expand their campuses. Ideally, we would have data on patterns of neighborhood change around university campuses, as we do for revitalization programs carried out by other institutions. Failing that, by examining patterns of neighborhood change around comparable urban-located research universities, and combining those data with studies of significant cases of change, we can assess how similar the Penn/West Philadelphia case is to those of other communities whose futures are entwined with the development of universities or similar institutions. However, with Penn as the flagship for this type of work in many ways, outcomes and metrics of change and renewal are even more difficult to find in other projects given their status.

Westfield State College president Evan Dobelle, author of the *Savior of Our Cities Survey*, provides a useful framework for evaluating and comparing what universities are doing in urban engagement. However, the criteria he gives are difficult to enumerate given how porous they are.[1] For example, Dobelle suggests that one criterion should be the length of community involvement programs, but involvement with a community may not be formal and is therefore not easily located in time. The informal nature of university–community relationships is not a negative. The social embeddedness of an institution through its informal relationships is actually something to encourage and support. The qualitative spirit of engagement is highly subjective and subject to debate within and beyond each institution mentioned in the survey. Expanded comparative research into the subject might take some of Dobelle's factors into consideration.

The cases in this chapter provide not a comprehensive comparative study of completed work but an exploratory meta-analysis of comparable institutions and the frameworks they have or are engaging in. For example, Columbia and Harvard are easily regarded as two of the best and richest schools in the nation. The University of Southern California and Northeastern University, although less wealthy and prestigious, are still, with comprehensive research and teaching, embedded in inner-city neighborhoods where their institutional aspirations are inhibited by their geographic and social contexts. In the case of Penn, Southern California, and Northeastern, there are factors tied to problems of local contexts and the urgency with which each institution sought to solve its problems. Columbia and Harvard also deal with problems of context, but these are not of the same scale, magnitude, or urgency as those of West Philadelphia, South Central Los Angeles, or the Roxbury neighborhood in Boston.

Columbia University

Earlier in the 2000s, the "roaring" of the Columbia Lion into the Manhattanville section of New York City attracted the attention and ire of nearby Harlem, for several reasons. The university's plan was to expand in a northwestern direction toward the George Washington Bridge, revitalizing industrial land for academic purposes.[2] There were several key differences between Columbia's and Penn's approaches to neighborhood revitalization. Most important, Columbia lacked a comparable social engagement and service infrastructure. Second, the university "in the City of New York" explicitly attempted to capture property for academic purposes. Most notably, the university claimed to be expanding its strengths in biotechnology research.[3]

The politics of land conveyance and speculation in New York exacerbates the tensions that would exist in any example. Columbia's topographical and historical social relationships with Harlem and Upper Manhattan are simply context for a bitter fight for land and dominance. Most important, a key difference between Columbia and Penn is the rhetorical frame constructed by each university around its real estate projects. In both cases, historical incidents do much of the framing for these institutions; however, Columbia's plans to expand make much less sense in the context of Upper Manhattan. The topography of West Harlem creates a natural boundary between Columbia and central Harlem that reinforces the exclusivity of and division between the two entities. The Metropolitan Transit Authority's subway line, which comes above ground at 120th Street and rises to an elevated line that towers over Manhattanville, creates yet another boundary that the university must cross. Columbia's health sciences campus in the Washington Heights neighborhood is markedly different. Not only is this campus completely severed from the contiguous section of the main campus; the demographics and social meaning of these spaces is drastically different as well.

Unlike Penn, Columbia's efforts at community engagement have been relatively low key, and this may have been by design. Columbia's failed attempt to construct a tiered gymnasium in the 1960s left a permanent stain on its relations with the Harlem community. This failure was memorialized in the student takeover of the campus in 1968, in which the communards of the Architecture program overtook Avery Hall specifically to protest the gymnasium plan. Their primary objections were to prospective access to the gym, which was to be built on city-owned land in Morningside Park. Columbia's privileged student clientele would enter through the western and higher elevation; Harlem's African American population would enter through the lower elevation in Harlem.[4]

Lee Bollinger's arrival as president of Columbia in 2002 brought with it several things, including an enhanced interest in moving forward on Manhattanville with a formal planning process. As with all universities, several key gaffes frustrated its plans and intentions, the most serious being the implication, and in some cases explicit assertion, that Manhattanville was "vacant" and underutilized.[5] Columbia's Manhattanville planning process included two major phases. The first is slated for completion by 2015 and will include new academic facilities for scientific research and several academic units, including the university's Business School, School of International and Public Affairs, and School of the Arts. Community benefits in this phase include two Columbia-supported public schools: a K–8 school to be directed by the Teacher's College and a high school that will focus on science, technology, and mathematics. The second phase is scheduled for completion in 2030 and will include additional academic space and housing for graduate students and faculty.

Of the cases presented here, Columbia's is simultaneously the most like and the most unlike Penn's. Both of their institutional contexts are challenged inner city communities. However, the boundaries between the campuses and the surrounding areas are different. More important, the stance of each institution toward its context paralleled the other's until the arrival and tenure of Seth Low at Columbia in 1890. Only when Martin Meyerson's presidency at Penn began in 1970 did that institution seem to appreciate its urban context in any way. And it was not until Rodin that a coherent agenda was formed and found institutional backing. Low's successor, Nicolas Murray Butler (1902–1945) reduced Low's urban focus and turned Columbia inward, but now the university is fully turning outward again. This turn, however, comes in conjunction with the university's expansion plans and the vociferous complaints from community residents, area business owners, students, and others. One example is Hudson Moving and Storage, whose facilities became a lightning rod in the Manhattanville project's execution. The university has now negotiated an agreement with the company to relocate its facilities temporarily while construction takes place around them. This has led to an agreement with a local church to assist in its relocation as well.

Columbia has been forced to compromise and formulate a response that indicated its willingness to concede that Manhattanville offers economic opportunities for local residents. It has negotiated and executed a Community Benefits Agreement with Harlem that specifies the economic and social impacts (i.e., benefits) for the community once the expansion is completed. A new version of the 1968 events occurred in November of 2007 when several students went on a hunger strike to protest the university's plans for Manhattanville. What is notable is the inclusion of Columbia-supported public schools, specific targets for employment, and clear statements from the university about local retail and its intention not to inhibit local entrepreneurs or tinker with the historical legacy and social fabric of Harlem.

By contrast, Penn's plans were far more opaque and unfolded only as needs, commentary, and institutional perspectives evolved. A network of somewhat loosely affiliated neighborhoods that are individually organized to varying degrees surrounds Penn, and they did not organize themselves to demand specific resources from the university. Columbia has had clear adversaries in vocal landowners, who have refused to sell, and in past Manhattan Borough president Ruth Messinger and current president Scott Stringer, who have echoed the concerns and complaints of Manhattan's Community Board 12.

Northeastern University

In a sea of highly respected institutions of higher education, Northeastern has grown into a major university worthy of the respect of its peers—with facilities to support that respect. From its glittering towers of steel and concrete, Northeastern students now look over the city of Boston as Harvard, MIT, and Boston University students do from their residential and academic towers. Founded in 1898 by a nearby Young Men's Christian Association (YMCA), the institution's original purpose was to offer evening classes to the men who lodged at YMCA. It evolved into a regional school that served as a ladder to the middle-class workforce and finally into the comprehensive research university it is today. It now draws students from across the country and has shifted its focus to accommodate more full-time students and an on-campus residential system.

However, Northeastern is faced with difficulties, one of which is geography. To its north and east are the Fenway area, the Museum of Fine Arts, and Symphony Hall; to its west and south are neighboring Wentworth Institute of Technology and now demolished public housing; and to the east lie both an obstacle and tremendous asset, one of the city's busiest rapid transit stations/bus transfer points. Expansion in any direction would prove challenging, expensive, or impossible. The easiest and fastest method would be to improve, enhance, and increase the density of facilities on land that the university already owned. As with Southern California and Penn, crime was and continues to be a problem for the institution, but this is largely because of significant contrasts each face of the university confronts. Northeastern's campus in many ways is the nexus of several different neighborhoods, with none of them recognizing the role the university plays in bringing these disparate and wildly divergent areas together.

To have its physical space match its new profile, the university has engaged in the simultaneous renovation of its campus and the construction of new housing immediately adjacent to it to improve the area's housing stock. The university's key off-campus project was Davenport Commons, a mixed-use facility that would accommodate Northeastern students and staff and the community.[6] The importance of this project, as a heuristic device, is that it was vigorously supported by the university but not driven entirely by it, and that the university openly admitted its inability to structure and manage a need for additional affordable housing for the Roxbury community.

Northeastern's push to build Davenport Commons was unique because it was inspired by city leaders eager to have its many colleges and universities build more student housing and ease competition in Boston's then-overheated rental market. Instead of aggressively and covertly acquiring property adjacent to its campus, Northeastern was approached by Boston Mayor Thomas Menino about purchasing a surface parking lot that the city had been unable to sell or convey to any other interested party. However, the mayor feared the reprisal of community groups who would interpret such a proposal as an effort to prioritize the university's needs over the low-income and predominantly African American and Latino Roxbury.

Unlike many of the universities discussed in this chapter, as well as Penn, there are some schools that partner with neighborhood community development corporations (CDCs) and neighborhood associations and marshal feedback on their designs and conceptual plans but drive and finance the project from beginning to end. Northeastern initiated the project but quickly stepped back to allow the local CDC, with a proven track record of fiscal responsibility and success in project management, to complete it. The CDC hired area residents as construction workers and encouraged local residents to move into the completed Davenport Commons. Moreover, Northeastern did not rely only on a highly effective CDC to drive the project but created a new organization that merged the Madison Park Development Corporation and two real estate organizations to organize the financing of affordable housing.

For its own campus development, the university designed a plan to expand and upgrade its housing and student-focused facilities. The "West Campus Development" plan called for an increase in the number of living units with groundbreaking architecture and novel services for an increasingly on-campus student population.[7] At one point, Northeastern prided itself on being the largest private university in the nation. A large commuting population that was only loosely tethered to the campus bolstered its claim.

The university's gaffe in accidentally revealing details of the Davenport Commons project before it was ready for public comment unleashed the first wave of opposition, even though media accounts of Northeastern's troubles with Roxbury pale in comparison to the challenges other communities have presented to comparable plans. The issue, as in so many places, was not the plans or designs themselves but the process through which they were revealed.[8] The lack of transparency appears to have been the university's greatest mistake.

University of Southern California

USC's relationship with South Central Los Angeles has defined it almost as much as West Philadelphia has defined Penn. Its most recent project, the University Park Campus (UPC) master plan, involves the revitalization of areas surrounding the campus, the upgrading of streetscapes, and the construction of 5,600 units of student housing with faculty housing a possibility. The impetus for this project appears to have come mostly from the need to grow the university by expanding academic and residential space, to increase safety on and near campus, and to encourage investment in the areas surrounding it.

USC's geographic location in relation to other parts of Los Angeles has always been both a part of its identity and a source of confusion for itself and area residents. Given its relative proximity to downtown Los Angeles, USC has throughout its history often sought to connect to downtown as a southern anchor of sorts. At the same time, it is at the northern edge of South Central Los Angeles, which the Los Angeles City Council has renamed in an attempt to eliminate popular references to an area known internationally for gang violence and inner-city decay. Students often joke that the acronym "USC" stands for the "University of South Central."[9]

Still, the institution brings a distinct identity to its surrounding area. The University Park campus sits in what many regard as a neighborhood of the same name. Immediately south is the Los Angeles Coliseum (the only stadium to have hosted two separate Olympic Games, the first in 1932 and the second in 1984) and the park grounds that surround it. On the northwest end of campus are the California African American Museum and the Shrine Auditorium, known for hosting the Academy Awards, the Grammys, and other high-profile media events. As well, a considerable amount of retail fronts the campus on one side or another.

Despite having recently passed the city's environmental impact review, many South Los Angeles residents are unhappy with the UPC, which has essentially been under way for the past eight years.[10] The primary issues revolve around the fate of retailers in the University Village retail mall. At the center of concern, in a direct parallel to the Penn case, is the Superior supermarket—which has a bilingual staff and serves a cross-section of ethnic and racial groups residing near the campus.[11] Focus groups convened by the university revealed that students, faculty, and staff wanted greater retail options. And they were not alone. Tenant business owners of the existing University Village complex wanted better retail options as well. The concern was whether tenants would be able to return to the newly rebuilt University Village after construction.[12] As in West Philadelphia, entrepreneurs who locate near universities draw upon students, university employees, and visitors for revenue. Such enterprises become difficult when universities control ground leases and set standards for retail outlets or operate those outlets themselves.

There are several burgeoning issues with the UPC plan. First, housing affordability is a challenge for both students and incumbent neighbors. As the connections between downtown Los Angeles and the USC campus are strengthened, housing prices are likely to increase. Also, as current rents in new housing near the USC campus demonstrate, the rehabilitation of the area's housing stock may exacerbate the challenges students face in securing nearby safe, quality, affordable housing. These changes to the local housing stock and potential changes to area retail present challenges for residents of the University Park and South Central Los Angeles neighborhoods. The university's commitment to public service and outreach may run counter to its master planning process, which seeks to improve USC's physical context and campus for its own institutional development.

Harvard University

"Seldom does an urban university have the opportunity to plan for decades of growth adjacent to its current campus and in the process also transform a neighborhood, enrich a local community, and contribute to the social, economic, and environmental development of a city." —Allston Development Group, *The Plan for Harvard in Allston*[13]

Harvard's relationship to Boston and Cambridge has been complex almost from the school's founding. Its acquisition of a forty-eight-acre parcel in the Allston neighborhood in 1997 changed its future geographic tilt from Cambridge toward Boston. This expansion, which is not yet complete, attempts to sidestep the problem of acquiring land and expanding around the university's historic center of Harvard Square by shifting expansion toward Harvard Stadium, the Business School, and graduate dormitories.

The original Allston plan calls for the migration of all or some of the Graduate School of Education from Cambridge and the School of Public Health from the Longwood medical area, a $1 billion science complex, and a number of undergraduate dormitories. It also calls for the construction of a university-owned art museum located at an intersection known as "Barney's Corner." The financial downturn has placed some of these projects in doubt, although the university is committed to fully developing the site in the future.

Championed vocally by former Harvard president Lawrence Summers, the plan has been deliberately slowed down by current president Drew Faust.[14] It would appear that there are several reasons for this. First, many of the early critiques of individual projects such as the art museum suggested that the university had not seriously considered residents' concerns over designs and placement. The sheer scale of the project would dwarf everything around it in a low-rise residential community. Second, the movement of academic units and undergraduate dormitories would disrupt the cohesion of undergraduate life and interdisciplinary activity on campus. With Harvard's strong tradition of undergraduate residential life, the splitting of facilities between Cambridge and Allston would threaten to alter this formula permanently.

Perhaps the most significant and instructive reason for the slowdown is the economic crisis itself. Between 2007 and 2009, Harvard's gargantuan endowment lost nearly one-third of its value, and university real estate holdings represented a considerable proportion of that loss. As of June 2009, the value of the university's real estate portfolio decreased by 50 percent, to $5 billion. In response, all construction in Allston was halted and the university moved to sell stakes in $1.5 billion of its real estate portfolio for cash.[15] For the sake of comparison, it is useful to understand that at the end of 2009 only twelve U.S. institutions had endowments totaling $5 billion or more. So for any institution to hold a portfolio of any asset that equals more than that is astonishing and speaks to the ease with which Harvard could acquire valuable Boston real estate for its campus expansion.

A notable difference between Harvard's approach to campus expansion and that of its peers is the lack of outward deference to a longer history of tensions between university and community. Harvard's footprint in Allston extends back to the turn of the twentieth century, when the university's stadium was erected there in 1903. The construction of the Business School in the neighborhood close to a decade later sealed the relationship. *The Plan for Allston* calls for the creation of an interdisciplinary campus that brings the Graduate School of Education and the School of Public Health together, faces the community at Barney's corner, and simultaneously connects the historic Cambridge campus to the Longwood Medical area. Pedestrian bridges will connect the Cambridge campus to the Allston campus's 9 million square feet of academic, athletic, and public space.

Of the four plans reviewed here, Harvard's is the least committal in both its future use of buildings and the potential benefits for the Allston community and the larger city of Boston. Its executive summary presents figures for potential long-term employment with the university and annual jobs generated by construction projects. However, given the opaque nature of building use proposals and ongoing issues with easements and property conveyance with existing landowners (e.g., CSX Transportation) several features of the plan may require much more time to fully realize, if they ever happen at all. Moreover, Harvard plans to build a new campus on industrial land that faces the residential areas of Allston in only a few discrete places and the Charles River in others. Although this provides little room for community opposition, the university has hosted several opportunities for community feedback and input.

Commonalities and Lessons

The schools discussed in this chapter share the common experience of seeing the land around their campuses devalued. The processes of decline can be traced to various factors, including but not limited to crime, unemployment, neighborhood disinvestment, and white flight. What these institutions share is the almost routine negative reaction to their plans to engage in neighborhood renewal and campus expansion and a common thread of distrust that runs through each case. As discussed earlier, there are victory stories of institutions that have worked around and through tensions with neighboring communities. On that score, one institution in particular stands out: Northeastern, which is assisting a local CDC with the construction of affordable off-campus housing. Northeastern had a strong interest in seeing the land around its campus increase in value and contribute to a sense of safety and livability. Its own account and collateral accounts that documented the project clearly place the CDC as the lead agency in the Davenport Commons housing development. The university was able to facilitate the conveyance of the land to the CDC and offer financial support that the CDC otherwise might not have obtained.

Therefore, the issue of credit in revitalization is not an insignificant one. However, local history, local context, and institutional legacy matter as well. The approaches that the schools discussed here have taken to community revitalization, campus expansion, and improvement are varied; however, some common themes emerge. In the cases of USC and Penn, their surroundings demanded their attention. Both institutions developed large-scale infrastructures for community engagement, service learning, and institutional support of local communities. Large-scale plans for improvement and/or expansion of their campuses were developed much later and in both cases were tethered to the universities' narratives of service and altruism. In the case of Columbia, there was a clear break in the university's mission, identity, and commitment to its urban environment. One perspective is that the timing of the revival of its formal branding as the university "in the City of New York," and collateral from that, followed the negative reactions to its preliminary plans for the expansion of its Morningside Heights campus into Manhattanville. The suggestion in those early plans that this land was underutilized flew in the face of the lessons Northeastern learned in the development of Davenport Commons. Without figures such as Harkavy and Rodin, plans for campus expansion and development appear as opportunistic land grabs with no real or suggested benefits for adjacent communities.

Penn and Northeastern stand out in that they initiated their campus development plans by leveraging their long histories of community engagement and service and by committing to more of the same moving forward. In contrast, original plans for Columbia's Manhattanville project called for a jazz restaurant/nightclub near the center of the new campus. This "homage" to Harlem reflected a total dissonance with what Harlem had become and with what jazz music now is and who listens to it, and it further stood as a marker of how disconnected Columbia's planners were from the university's local context. Subsequent plans dropped any mention of such an establishment.

Conversely, Harvard did not alter its community engagement strategy leading up to the announcement of its Allston plans; nor did it do so afterward. Columbia's and Harvard's resources, prestige, and relative isolation from problematic inner-city communities are factors that cannot be ignored. Penn, Northeastern, and USC had to "rush" to engage campus improvements and neighborhood conditions, as these directly affected their somewhat "elastic" goods. That is, Harvard and Columbia might not be what they are if they were located where Penn, Northeastern, and USC are located, but, even if they were, the opportunity to study or work at either Columbia or Harvard would trump a desire to avoid their urban contexts. Thus, institutional aspirations might play a distinct role in how colleges and universities decide to engage in urban neighborhood revitalization and campus expansion.

Universities are not monolithic; they contain a multitude of agents who are interested (or uninterested) in community engagement, campus expansion, and neighborhood revitalization. A clear common factor is institutional leadership. As with Rodin and Gutmann at Penn and other university leaders not discussed here, such as Ruth Simmons at Brown and the former president of Case Western Reserve University, Edward Hundart, support for urban engagement comes from the top of the organization and resources are realigned accordingly. Constituencies previously recalcitrant and uncooperative come along to support the new paradigm in university leadership.

Ziona Austrian and Jill S. Norton provide a useful framework for understanding university real estate investment, in which development decisions are driven by two sets of factors.[16] Independent factors include motivation, physical environment, policy oversight, and leadership. Dependent factors include the decision-making process, types of real estate projects, financing mechanisms, and university–community relations. My friendly amendment to their framework is to embed it entirely in the sociological analysis of neighborhood change. More concretely, university decision makers—or those interested in shaping the university's opinions and actions—should consider what the longer-term impacts of university-driven real estate development might be. If successful, programs to support public education, affordable housing and housing enhancement programs, historic preservation of neighborhood institutions, and workforce development can have transformative effects on places. The balancing of place-based and incumbent-raising revitalization efforts is complex, nuanced, and hard to define or measure. Columbia's plans for Manhattanville are far from fruition, but perhaps, among the plans reviewed here, they may have the greatest potential to transform Upper Manhattan and provide the greatest benefit to area residents. The existence of the Community Benefits Agreement provides a paper trail with which to assess the university's progress and effectiveness.

Harvard's *Plan for Allston* is equivalent to Northeastern's West Campus Development initiative, Penn's East Campus expansion, Columbia's Manhattanville expansion, and the University of Southern California's master planning effort in the University Park neighborhood—all borrow from Penn's playbook without paying homage.

And that is most likely in part because of the confounding of Penn's longer-term effort to revitalize and transform the neighborhoods to its west as it prepared to move eastward. These efforts were separate and distinct, separated by time, presidential administrations, market conditions, and the university's successes in West Philadelphia. This is not a small point, and it speaks directly to what universities do and how their neighbors may react.

USC's planning effort is among the most nascent of those discussed here. The university's long history of community service and engagement becomes juxtaposed to the current master planning process rather than complementary to a measure intended to serve both community *and* university. What is often lost on observers of the Penn-driven renewal in West Philadelphia is that the university itself underwent massive improvements and transformations at the same time. If anything was covert, it was what the university was doing to itself and not to the community.

In Chapter 6, I discuss the many questions and challenges both universities and adjacent communities must answer to move the dialogue forward. As I discuss, the answers are not in the plans but in the explicit intentions and aspirations of both.

6

Conclusion

Lessons from West Philadelphia

I f a university engages in neighborhood improvement and gentrification results, does the university become a villain or a hero?
The literature on community development provides few examples of community development and upgrading that do not coincide
with gentrification and displacement of the incumbent population
in some form, albeit at times welcomed by some residents. There are
also nagging questions about transparency and accountability. Should
universities be responsible for urban revitalization? Moreover, how
do we amend future university-driven planning efforts, particularly
when precedents have had negative outcomes? This final chapter
speaks to these issues and summarizes the lessons that other institutions and cities may want to take from Penn's work.

Here I provide an overview of the university as a complex variable in urban neighborhood change. On a broad scale, I examine the
relationship between all universities and their host cities. On a nar-
rower scale, I look at the history of urban-located research universities in the United States and the evolving roles they have adopted
(and eschewed) over time. Each role, and the extent to which universities have effectively played it, has had an impact on urban

development and social life. To illuminate this history, I discuss the "how" and "why" of the complex relationship between cities and their higher education sector and its impacts. I also discuss the implications of the latest iterations for both.

In the history of many of the world's leading institutions of higher education there has always been a connection to urban life. Since their beginnings, U.S. cities and their universities have changed both independently and interdependently. The long evolution of higher education entails an array of institutional types. A fundamental difference between the history of the university in the United States and that in Europe has been the university's mission and its relationship to its geographic (urban) surroundings. In both settings, this history has been symbiotic and frequently conflictive depending on the university in question.

Despite the popularity of terms such as "town–gown," which evoke persistent conflict between the "town" and the college or university, this chapter suggests that the relationship between cities and universities is historically one of convergence, of which traditional and popular tensions over nuisances such as loud and unruly college students is but one aspect. Convergence has roots in the contemporary commercialization of all aspects of urban life and higher education. Under the current paradigm of neoliberal market ideology, both town and university have pursued fulfillment of their traditionally not-for-profit missions with for-profit management schemes. In a few, municipalities or metropolitan regions and higher education have found common interest in economic development and now local neighborhood redevelopment.

The historical relationship between higher education and cities has not been static. Universities in the United States have changed drastically from the early colonial liberal arts colleges of their beginnings into the mega-research-commercial and nearly autonomous political authorities they are today.[1] While many popular conceptions of modern universities include legends of great stored wealth, unilateral decision making, and unified mission and direction, the reality is that many are poorly funded, ill-managed, chaotic, and internally conflicted. In fact, these institutions may support regional economic development simply through the production of large numbers of graduates who feed local labor markets.

Research universities must respond not only to demands that they serve the public interest but also to economic and fiscal demands to compete with other universities in a number of ways. The withdrawal of state-level fiscal support for higher education means that public universities have become entrepreneurial and must become much more so. Private universities without a need for state-level appropriations compete more intensely for wealthy students and talented faculty.

I have identified two salient roles that universities play in cities. The first is as a driver of economic development; the second is as a real estate developer. In my discussion of the response of universities to the urban crisis of the 1960s and 1970s is an implicit description of a third role—university as community partner or service provider. I suggest here that all universities have played all of these roles or some subset of them—and doing so has had implications for their host communities. For urban communities, the engagement of colleges and universities represents opportunities to leverage some of the only significant fixed capital still found in inner-city neighborhoods. For universities, this engagement represents many things, the least of which is an opportunity to rehabilitate their urban contexts that have in some cases followed a slide of forty years or more into near total blight and abandonment. This convergence of interests between higher education and development interests beyond university walls has significant impacts on how planners and policy makers understand changing urban neighborhoods in the current era.

The Evolving Industry of Higher Education

Between the conclusion of the War for Independence and the founding of many of this country's cities and institutions of higher learning, capitalist production evolved significantly. By the end of the nineteenth century, U.S. cities—particularly those in the Northeast and the northern Midwest—were highly industrialized.[2] This rise of industrial capitalism paralleled a shift in the mission of higher education, which mirrored the challenge issued by Wilhelm von Humboldt that led to the establishment of the University of Berlin in 1810.[3] In the United States, the Morrill Act married Humboldt's utilitarian view of higher education with the development of the agricultural economy.[4]

This stands in contrast to the role that universities historically played in Europe. Thomas Bender writes that the purpose of early European universities and many of those that emerged during the Middle Ages was to be a "community of scholars that preserved religious knowledge."[5] Sometimes, too, the university granted status, authority, and access to privileged positions in society.[6] Similarly, the founders of Harvard College in 1636 sought to ensure that men of faith were present in all trades and professions.[7] Other early university founders in America such as Benjamin Franklin, who chartered the University of Pennsylvania, sought to raise the profile of their cities and towns and establish institutions that would train youth in the "practical arts."[8]

The European tradition of being *in* and *of* the city differed from that of colonial colleges, which sought more bucolic and sylvan campus settings.[9] In many cases, the actual leadership of these institutions attempted to divorce the college from the city in an aim to protect students from the city's "vices and temptations." In the nineteenth and early twentieth centuries, Columbia and the University of Pennsylvania, for example, moved their campuses to other locations in New York and Philadelphia, respectively, in an effort to remove themselves from the distractions of their cities' central districts.[10] The desire to construct universities in relative seclusion from their urban and "immoral" surroundings resonates with the ideas espoused by John Henry Newman in the nineteenth century and the founders of many of the nation's earliest colleges and universities.[11] Newman's book, *Idea of a University*, was not just a blueprint but also a response to Victorian critics who charged the university with having lost touch with reality.

The historical context of universities' antiurban bias throughout the twentieth century includes the processes of urbanization and deindustrialization. As the industrial base of many northern and northeastern cities began to crumble in mid-century, thousands of jobs and middle-class families migrated to the suburbs. Simultaneously, large numbers of African Americans continued their migration northward to take advantage of economic opportunities and to escape overt racism in the South.[12] The confluence of these historical events was the beginning of the urban crisis.

Almost a century before the onset of the urban crisis, many felt that cities were the ideal locations for institutions of higher learning. The antecedents for the events that brought us to this moment in history came to cities and universities before World War II. A good deal of the technology that drove innovation during this era was, at least in theory, connected to the products of university research.[13] The late nineteenth century also saw the rise of the "land grant" university, which was designed to bring aid to the agricultural hinterlands of America and provide practical education to youth in those regions.[14] This role for universities affirmed the Baconian and Humboldtian ideal of a university that supports the "estate of man" and the progress of the state.[15] The emergence of institutions such as the Massachusetts Institute of Technology (MIT), which was founded in Boston's Back Bay neighborhood and not its current Cambridge location, was not a historical accident. As early as 1869, MIT president, Charles Eliot stated,

> A technological school is best placed in a large city in a great industrial center within easy reach of works, mills, forges, machine shops, and mines. The professors of a scientific school have need to be brought into daily contact with practical affairs, to watch the progress of new inventions as they develop from day to day, and to know the men who are improving special industries. The students of a scientific school have a like need.[16]

Because of the role MIT came to play in the development of Boston and New England, it, and institutions like it, become important in chronicling the relationship between higher education and cities. The development of schools like MIT signaled a movement toward an applied and practical focus within the academy. Without question, these schools represent an archetype for the successful leveraging of a university and the knowledge it produces for economic growth. This perspective became prologue to the role that such institutions played in buoying the struggling New England economy in the late twentieth century.

During the economic restructuring of cities in the postwar period, the field of higher education changed in several ways. For one, many states created urban extensions of their large land grant universities. Rutgers, the University of Wisconsin–Milwaukee, the University of Massachusetts–Boston, and the University of Illinois–Chicago are but a few examples of schools created with explicit urban missions. Their purpose was to educate the growing numbers of students in cities for whom traditional U.S. residential college life was an unlikely option.[17] These institutions were in many cases like the University of Wisconsin–Milwaukee, which was formed through a reorganization and merger of the larger University of Wisconsin's Urban Extension department and the Wisconsin Teacher's College.[18] Their expressed missions were to complete the democratic promise of American higher education.[19]

In some ways, these institutions followed in the tradition of Franklin, John Dewey, Seth Low of Columbia, and others who sought to ensure that their institutions, and higher education generally, remained connected to the societies in which they found themselves. The university's value to society was its ability to draw inspiration for learning and knowledge creation from the city itself. The challenge for the successors of Franklin, Dewey, Low, and others has been to find ways to live up to these pragmatic ideals for higher education and still remain competitive in an emerging higher education marketplace. This transition included an intense competition for prestige and often external support. In describing the evolution of Columbia, Bender writes that, in its attempt to join the elite institutions of the nation, the university liberated its disciplines to "develop in increasing isolation from the city . . . the university increasingly looked to the nation, not the city as its context."[20] In post–World War II New York, three major institutions had missions of service to the city. The

City College of New York offered to instruct the masses of the city's poor. New York University promised to cater to its middle classes and provide instruction in "practical arts" in a manner consistent with the goal of the University of London. "Columbia University in the City of New York," as it is formally known, sought to serve the nation and withdraw from the city.

Benjamin Franklin's peers on the University of Pennsylvania's board of trustees did not wait for his death to betray him. They intended to create a liberal arts institution that mimicked the curriculum of rival institutions such as Harvard.[21] Penn has come a long way from being the first institution to call itself *university* to becoming a research powerhouse and one of the world's leading universities. Contemporary colleges and universities are no longer the sleepy tax-exempt academic guilds of the nineteenth century; they are expected to push the profitable knowledge-driven growth in science and technology needed by competitive metropolitan regions. Penn has emerged as an institution capable of meeting that mandate.

The research powerhouses that dominated Cold War research funding after World War II are quite different from the urban universities created to accommodate the thousands of GIs returning from it. Attendance at the nation's universities was facilitated by the federal government's tuition assistance plan. Furthermore, the growing population of underserved urban poor, for whom sequestered residential college life was an unlikely option, contributed to an increase in student enrollments across the country. Contrary to popular opinion, the gulf between public and private research universities is increasing, not decreasing. Declining federal and state support and the virtual extinction of municipally supported institutions has forced a majority of postsecondary schools to compete with elites that benefit from their historical linkages to the federal government, industry, and the social elites of their host cities and the nation.

In many cases, the metropolitan areas with major research institutions that plugged into the government largesse for Cold War research have far surpassed those whose universities did not. Regions wishing to compete with places such as Silicon Valley and Route 128 in Massachusetts have had to play a game of catch-up.[22] The presence of research institutions also attracts a cadre of young, talented workers to their host cities not only for work opportunities but also for continued learning, spouse trailing, and the like. These cities have also benefited from the service businesses that are attracted by high-growth industries.

Despite the boom enjoyed by New England and Silicon Valley resulting from the knowledge spillovers created by institutions such as MIT and Stanford, few regions fully realized the potential for dynamic economic growth until the late 1990s.[23] All institutions contribute to local development in one way or another through their employment and local purchasing. However, some, like many large and complex research universities, are capable of contributing much more through the volume and transferability of their research.

Universities and Their Evolving Leadership

Another way in which universities have evolved is in their leadership. Contemporary college and university presidents are expected to achieve more than their predecessors. Clark Kerr cites the risks of having a "star" faculty less interested in pedagogical issues and undergraduate education than in the portability of their careers and resources.[24] The past fifteen years have also seen the ascendance of the "star" university president alongside his or her star faculty. More than mere fundraisers or figureheads, these individuals are significant figures; presidential searches and resignations are now front-page news.[25]

Internally, a university president's role as head of an increasingly entrepreneurial enterprise is worthy of scholarly attention. Education sociologist Burton Clark refers to the ability of presidents to transform the internal mechanisms and structures of a university as "steering capacity." Clark suggests five pathways to institutional transformation; chief among them is creating a strengthened steering core.[26] He does not speak specifically to the role of president, but university chief executives play a substantial role in creating such transformation.

It is useful to combine Clark's analysis with the notion of "crisis." In his brief analysis, Clark mentions universities that fear marginal status and might be poised to induce their own transformation. A more direct catalyst for action is a crisis that demands change—fiscal, administrative, programmatic, or curricular. As Taylorist-type organizations, universities have explicit and often rigid divisions of labor, which can make coordination of quasi-autonomous academic units difficult.[27] Currently, the "star" university president is the one who can steer his or her institution through a crisis, manage it to respond to public expectations or to those of its various constituencies, and realign the divisions of labor to make the institutions more efficient.

Universities and the Demands of Their Student Clientele

Despite record numbers of applications to many elite colleges and universities, the competition for the most diverse and selective students rose exponentially in the 1990s and continues to grow. In the pursuit of wealthy and talented applicants, some elite schools have resorted to discounting tuition and developing high-end campus amenities. Observers have criticized these institutions for their pursuit of wealthy students at the expense of students from low-income families. Critics argue that the competition to lure top students with exorbitant luxuries is driving up the costs of higher education and making an exclusive resource that much more exclusive.[28]

This commentary is relevant to my research on the relationship between higher education and its urban contexts because many colleges and universities are now more concerned than ever with their urban environments, which they see as extensions of the amenities they themselves offer and control. This, of course, goes well beyond concerns over crime and public safety. Yale's redevelopment and management of more than eighty retail stores near its campus has helped spur a small renaissance in its hometown of New Haven,[29] but this effort has not been without controversy. The relative lack of diversity in shopping choices reflects Yale University Properties' penchant for high-end retail outlets and its assumption they will be more attractive to "preppy" students and comparable consumers.[30]

Universities Respond to the Urban Crisis

The urban crisis of the mid-twentieth century resulted from the confluence of three distinct events. First, U.S. cities in the rust belt—the Northeast and northern Midwest—underwent rapid economic restructuring. Entry-level manufacturing jobs migrated to spacious and racially homogenous suburbs, just as large numbers of African Americans continued their migration northward to take advantage of economic opportunities and escape the South.[31] Battles over residential and school desegregation exacerbated the problem by prompting the emigration of middle-class whites, leaving the desperately poor behind in inner-city neighborhoods. This group of desperately (and chronically) poor has been termed "the underclass" by urban sociologists and other social scientists.

For a great while, many institutions turned their backs to cities and allowed the decline of industry and neighborhoods to continue unabated. The story of the Association of Urban Universities, as told by J. B. Crooks, chronicles the challenges faced by a number of institutions that attempted to serve the needs of rapidly expanding urban populations.[32] In time, that mission would conflict with the need to pursue support from the federal government and industry for basic and advanced research. The response to the urban crisis of colleges and universities in American cities was as varied as the institutions and cities themselves. The effectiveness of their interventions is debatable and relative depending on the particular problems of the cities they were trying to help.

Regardless of what universities and their leadership attempted to do for cities in response to the urban crisis, it is clear that they had a stake in improving their surrounding communities. Crime and blight threatened the ability of many to attract and retain talented faculty and students, and endangered the vitality of their academic villages. Rising crime on and around several university campuses, including the University of Chicago, Pennsylvania, and Yale, inspired those schools to take action. In this way, engagement was tied to the preservation of university interests. Armed with the language of advocacy and participatory planning, many universities engaged their communities with the intent of saving themselves and creating places that were more attractive to students, faculty, and private investment. Critiques of "rational" comprehensive planning in the 1960s and 1970s gave rise to pluralistic, participatory, and advocacy planning processes.[33]

Just as with federal contracting for research, universities did not respond to the needs of their communities in the same ways. By virtue of their geographic location within cities, and the intentions that belied their founding principles, they often developed responses that varied as much as they did. In the postwar period, many universities were more concerned with expanding to accommodate new waves of college enrollment brought about by the GI Bill and the dramatic increases in women and minorities now pursuing higher education.[34] To grow the campuses physically, many schools in urban areas took advantage of the 1961 Section 112 Amendment to the Housing Act of 1949, which allowed cities or nonprofit entities to seize blighted areas and properties and redevelop them for institutional use.[35] The record of university engagement in a federal policy for seizing land to eradicate neighborhood "blight" and promote redevelopment is a controversial and complicated one that has racial undertones. The residue of higher education's role in urban renewal and in the displacement of low-income neighborhoods near campuses is still remarkably close to the surface of university–community relations.

The failure of higher education to play a more significant role in the resolution to the urban crisis, in conjunction with decreases in funding, forced many institutional leaders to question whether urban service missions were appropriate for universities.[36] Such questioning led to the 1977 disbanding of the Association of Urban Universities, whose inability to maintain an urban-focused mission at the veritable height of the urban crisis speaks to the commitment of higher education to the public interest.

One outgrowth of the work of urban universities has been the many variations of university–community partnerships that focus specifically on issues such as public safety, public education reform, community economic development, homeownership, and affordable housing. These are only a few examples; however, they show that most university–community partnerships were created with the idea that the university should leverage its resources to aid cities and communities. These partnerships are no longer limited to urban service-oriented institutions, but now have found advocates in all institutional types, particularly some of the more prestigious such as the University of Pennsylvania. Over time, universities have formed mutually beneficial partnerships with communities, which have transformed schools, reduced crime, created affordable housing, and established access to health care.[37] Still, the notion of "enlightened self-interest" has become a socially acceptable way of integrating a politically progressive movement designed to assist the city's poor and needy with the broader interests of universities.[38]

These more sophisticated partnerships have not completely escaped criticism.[39] In a tone similar to that of the debates that finally killed the AUU, Howell Baum asks if universities promise to deliver more to urban communities than they can possibly deliver. He observes that the promise of university engagement brings with it the imprimatur of expertise, resources, and prestige, but in too many cases the good intentions of ideologically progressive faculty and administrators lead to an attempt to "solve the problems of a troubled school district with two graduate assistants in one semester."[40]

Universities as Drivers of Economic Growth

A great deal of the most recent writing on universities as catalysts for growth is steeped in regional economic development interests. Thus, great importance is given to the quality of an institution and its ability to attract and retain talent. Converting basic scientific research into profitable technology, businesses, and royalties for the researcher and institution that produced it is also central to an analysis of the role of universities in economic growth.[41] Many researchers focus on the success of a few institutions in specific regions, with little regard for the myriad of complex factors that led to the dynamic economic growth they describe. In most cases, the relationships between cities/regions and their institutions of higher education can be summarized by a careful examination of the multifaceted economic, political, social, and legal ties between each institution and its host.

Contrary to the various reports issued by private think tanks, and by universities themselves, the economic benefits of a university presence (generally) are not well documented.[42] Recent studies suggest that the "backward"—that is, indirect—economic benefits of a research university may be in large part a result of the local spending patterns of the institution, its faculty, staff, and students. Because of the emphasis in discussions of the knowledge-driven economy, talent attraction and retention, and the creative class, still ascendant in the United States, economic development professionals are looking to colleges and universities as the instruments that will help transform their marginal cities and regions into Silicon Valley or Route 128.

The role of universities as drivers of economic development is not played solely at the regional level. Over the past twenty years, many have come to better understand how universities support local businesses as well. Traditionally, the impacts of a university on local merchants and vendors have been seen as the result of spending by students, faculty, and staff. Moreover, universities, as corporate entities, consume massive amounts of products, materials, and services. Local purchasing programs have strengthened the economic relationship between universities and their venders and service providers in immediate and adjacent neighborhoods.

This discussion involves an increasing need for universities to secure outside support for research and, to a lesser extent, teaching. The founders of the Massachusetts Institute of Technology and the original beneficiaries of the Morrill Act were in line with the Franklinesque ideals of "practical education" and the Humboldtian mandate that universities advance the progress of the state.[43] The urban location of many American universities promotes the realization of these ideals. Without their locations, the rich environments for applied research, service learning for students, and rich and broad labor markets from which to recruit staff and faculty, many universities would have trouble fulfilling their missions or competing in the industry of higher education.

Universities, particularly research universities, have come to realize how important robust regional economies are to their own technology transfer agendas. Cities and metropolitan regions not only are home to institutions but also represent a marketplace for university research.[44] In this era of commercializable research, universities must be located in metropolitan areas or they must create businesses that can absorb and commercialize the research they produce. Of course, this is related to the idea that these institutions can serve as catalysts for regional growth, as institutions such as MIT and Stanford have.

The Bayh-Dole Act of 1980 afforded higher education institutions (HEIs) the opportunity to pursue commercializable academic research and reap its financial rewards.[45] Commercial spin-offs can be the impetus for phenomenal regional growth by creating and building entirely new industries. The promise of information technology, engineering, biotechnology, and life science as engines of regional economic growth has been realized in many places where clusters of colleges and universities are located.

In recent years, most large research universities have issued economic impact reports that catalogue the benefits of their presence in a community.[46] These reports not only justify their nonprofit status at a time when this is increasingly coming into question, but also are a means of marshaling increased support from regional and national commercial interests.[47] The current building boom in higher education in response to growing student enrollments, increased research productivity, and university-based student services has created a need for more space. Moreover, for landlocked and immobile universities, this combination of pressures, incentives, and needs creates challenges and opportunities.

Universities as Real Estate Developers

A not so new, but largely unexplored, phenomenon is that of the university as landowner. In times of ever-decreasing state allocations for public higher education, near static federal subsidies have left the massive infrastructure of American higher education with a need to find new revenue streams.[48] For the most part, colleges, universities, and other nonprofit institutions such as hospitals and churches are exempt from property taxes as long as their property is being used to advance nonprofit activities. Recent profit-generating efforts by some institutions to establish high-end retail shops that service students, faculty, and staff, or to lease space to for-profit firms collaborating with university researchers, has not gone unnoticed by fiscally strapped towns and cities.

Historically, one of the most cited reasons for university-generated real estate development was the need to expand campuses in the post-World War II era. If the productive capacity of cities is on the decline as we head toward an "intellectual capitalism," the role of universities and knowledge producers will increase in importance. This is true not only in an economic sense; Columbia's current Manhattanville expansion project is centered on the university's need to expand its facilities for high-end research and to provide comparable amenities to its student body. By extension, its land use becomes a primary piece of evidence of what is happening to HEIs, their impacts on the larger society, and the social/economic order they help to reproduce.

In addition, many universities have engaged in real estate development in an effort to stabilize residential neighborhoods and commercial markets. Their tax-exempt status allows them to invest in real estate with less risk than a private investor might face. In some cases, property can become attractive simply because of the university's prestige. The captive audience of university students and faculty appeals to bookstores, coffee shops, and clothing retailers, among others. The imprimatur of the university's involvement itself bears some importance in the value of particular real estate developments. Universities acting as developers have been able to establish the standard for development and create markets for office space. In Princeton's case, the university's cachet not only helped attract business to the sleepy southern New Jersey corridor midway between New York City and Philadelphia, but also helped create a market for office space that had not previously existed.[49] Many for-profit knowledge-based companies, such as those in biotechnology and information technology, consider accessibility to a university and its intellectual resources an important draw. MIT and Stanford have served as magnets for the Boston and Silicon Valley areas, respectively, since the early twentieth century. The location of companies in, on, or near land owned or leased by a university generates revenue that supports other corners of the institution that do not yield similar monies.

Many institutions develop real estate for yet to be determined institutional use. Having learned their lessons from urban renewal, they now "bank" land to accommodate expansion in the years to come or, at the very least, to leverage it for resources somewhere down the road. Indeed, land is often more commercially valuable if it is not used for university purposes. For example, Columbia reluctantly accepted a gift in 1814 of the four blocks that would one day host the Lincoln Center for the Performing Arts.[50] This land remains a part of the university's endowment, which in the late 1980s represented two-thirds of the university's New York area real estate holdings.

In the race for student and faculty talent, many universities have transformed their campuses into "service centers" that can and do provide any conceivable type of service. Although enrollments at an increasing number of U.S. colleges and universities continue to climb, the amount of space needed has climbed faster—a fact that very little of the relevant literature has yet examined. Perhaps universities do need more land to accommodate broader academic missions. However, this chapter suggests that the acquisition of urban land to further enhance "urban utopias" in the form of campuses is connected to the commercialization of urban space and many aspects of higher education. Demands that higher education and the knowledge it produces advance the welfare of humankind require that society continually question how the field of education delivers on that obligation.

Summary

As U.S. cities continue to shift from centers of industrial production to service-oriented "knowledge centers," universities will remain critical to urban economic viability and social life. An issue not well studied is the historical, economic, and social trends that cause so many universities to develop in or near areas that are epicenters of urban poverty, crime, and blight. The lack of university investment in inner-city communities may contribute to these conditions, but there is no empirical evidence of a direct cause. Cities need their research universities, but are they as helped as harmed by them? Because of their nonprofit status and geographic position as fixed capital, universities exist with the expectation that they will advance the public's interest and welfare. The analysis in Chapter 4 suggests that urban neighborhoods may change for a variety of reasons. Despite their implicit public mission, urban universities must respond to a plethora of demands and pressures that often take precedence.

With the U.S. economy shifting from industrial production to knowledge production, the geographical importance of the university cannot be understated. This has important implications for how the university identifies itself. While many observers agree that universities were mostly established for the purpose of knowledge production, disagreement arises when we ask "how" that knowledge is produced and "what" type of knowledge results. Criticisms of the university have often failed to answer that question or to locate the university on a political map. For that reason, the research question on which any answer is based assumes a political-economic perspective.

The convergence of economic development interests in cities and universities points toward a noticeable gap in the discourse on "knowledge economies," "cities of knowledge," "learning societies," and so forth, as well as in the discourse on the relationship between universities, cities, and race and class. As has been well documented, antiurban bias in the United States became synonymous with "race" and "class" in the late nineteenth and twentieth centuries.[51] Antiurban sentiments among college and university students, faculty, leaders, and others reflected that association.

Universities are far too complex for such analyses. Instead, it may make more sense to consider how various university stakeholders influence university decision making, and how they may compete with each other to have influence on the surrounding community, city, and region. As Clark Kerr suggests, universities have already or will become "multiversities"—chaotic, unmanageable, and increasingly complex.[52] As a result, their relationship to their host cities will have to change.

The empirical study of contemporary campus expansion and real estate development is a means to a better understanding of how the university is divided and increasingly commercialized. The complementary ethnographic (and no less empirical) study of university–community relations as a part of expansion and development exposes the co-opting of the language of participation, representation, collaboration, and community development by university leaders to serve the interests of the research-extensive university.

The university's contemporary "awareness" of the importance of its connection with the city comes at a time when popular attention paid to the plight of the urban poor has faded and the push for universities to serve as catalysts of dynamic regional (and national) economic growth has never been greater. It also comes at a time in the history of U.S. higher education when competition for students, faculty, and research dollars (federal, private, industry) is as great as ever. That competition has been marked by the unprecedented physical growth of college and university campuses. For institutions confined to tight quarters in urban areas, the challenge of expanding without dredging up painful memories of urban renewal and the role of colleges and university in that legacy has been difficult.[53]

Cities need their colleges and universities, and these institutions need their cities. However, to what end? Perry suggests that they need each other not just for intellectual stimulation and external support but also to provide students with a stimulating environment to keep the knowledge they produce "grounded."[54] Universities withdraw from cities (and society) and/or engage them in irresponsible and damaging ways at their own peril. Greenwood argues that social embeddedness and social ties/obligations are somewhat clearer for public than for private institutions.[55] This is not to suggest that private institutions are exempt from public scrutiny, but it is plausible that they are free to compete with like institutions for talent, students, and the public support they enjoy through research grants and tax-exempt land.

As the preceding chapters show, a private research-oriented university's engagement in urban revitalization implicates the institution in the evolving geography of poverty, opportunity, and social exclusion. Characterizing a university's engagement in urban revitalization as simple self-interested real estate speculation is inaccurate and unfair. Despite the contemporary assumption that the university should or will operate for profit glosses over its complex and unique nature and that of the higher education sector at large. The data from the West Philadelphia/Penn case reveal a tangled web of market/political forces that compelled Penn to respond in particular ways that have had both positive and negative impacts on its neighboring communities.

Notes

PREFACE

1. Lisa Foderero, "Critics Turn out at an Open House on N.Y.U. Expansion," *New York Times*, April 14, 2010, available at http://www.nytimes.com/2010/04/15/nyregion/15nyu.html.

2. There are numerous universities in the cities mentioned, but the cases that are most similar to Penn's in each are Case Western Reserve, Johns Hopkins, the University of Southern California, Yale, and Ohio State.

3. See Peter Marris, *Loss and Change* (London: Routledge, 1986).

CHAPTER 1

1. Herbert Rubin, "Shoot Anything That Flies; Claim Anything That Falls: Conversations with Economic Development Practitioners," *Economic Development Quarterly* 2, no. 3 (1988): 236–251.

2. Robert A. Beauregard, *Voices of Decline: The Postwar Fate of US Cities* (Cambridge, MA: Blackwell, 1993). See also Paul S. Grogan and Tony Proscio, *Comeback Cities: A Blueprint for Urban Neighborhood Revival* (Boulder, CO: Westview Press, 2000); and, more recently, Alan Berube, "The State of Metropolitan America: Suburbs and the 2010 Census" Brookings Institution, July 14, 2011, http://www.brookings.edu/speeches/2011/0714_census_suburbs_berube.aspx.

3. For case studies of university involvement in urban development, consult David C. Perry and Wim Wiewel, *The University as Urban Developer* (Armonk, NY: M. E. Sharpe, 2005); also see John I. Gilderbloom and R. L. Mullins, Jr., *Promise and Betrayal: Universities and the Battle for Sustainable Urban Neighborhoods* (Albany: State University of New York Press, 2005).

4. The University of Pennsylvania is most commonly referred to as Penn. Throughout the book, I will most often refer to it as "Penn" but will use its full formal name where appropriate.

5. Praise for the university's West Philadelphia Initiatives has come from a variety of institutions and commentators. Beyond citations in academic literature, which are cited throughout the book, the university's efforts received awards from the Urban Land Institute and the American Institute of Architects in 2003. See *University of Pennsylvania Almanac*, December 16, 2003.

6. There are a plethora of editorials, commentaries, and accounts of the circumstances that led to the development of the West Philadelphia Initiatives. The most comprehensive available are John Kromer and Lucy Kerman, *West Philadelphia Initiatives: A Case Study in Urban Revitalization* (Philadelphia: University of Pennsylvania and Fels Institute of Government, 2005); and Judith Rodin, "The 21st Century Urban University: New Roles for Practice and Research," *Journal of the American Planning Association* 71, no. 3 (2005): 237–249. Throughout, I will primarily reference these two works and additional sources from local Philadelphia newspapers, the *Daily Pennsylvanian* (the University of Pennsylvania independent student paper), and the *University of Pennsylvania Almanac*.

7. Douglas S. Heckathorn, "Respondent-Driven Sampling: A New Approach to the Study of Hidden Populations," *Social Problems* 44, no.2 (1997): 174–199; see also Roger Sanjek, "Network Organization and Its Uses in Urban Ethnography," *Human Organization* 37, no. 3 (1978): 257–268.

8. Three examples of this literature are CEOs for Cities and Initiative for a Competitive Inner City, *Leveraging Colleges and Universities for Urban Economic Revitalization: An Action Agenda* (Boston: ICIC, 2002), available at http://www.ceosforcities.org/files/colleges_1.pdf; Perry and Wiewel, *The University as Urban Developer*; and Richard Florida and Wesley M. Cohen, "Engine or Infrastructure? The University Role in Economic Development," in *Industrializing Knowledge: University-Industry Linkages in Japan and the United States*, ed. Lewis M. Branscomb, Fumio Kodama, and Richard Florida (Cambridge, MA: MIT Press, 1999), 589–610.

9. June Manning Thomas, "Rebuilding Inner Cities: Basic Principles," in *The Inner City: Urban Poverty and Economic Development in the Next Century*, ed. Thomas Boston and Catherine Ross (New Brunswick, NJ: Transaction Publishers, 1999), 67–74.

10. For a discussion of political language, see Murray Edelman, "Political Language and Political Reality," *PS* 18, no. 1 (Winter 1985): 10–19.

11. For more on this quote, see David W. Bartelt, "Renewing Center City Philadelphia: Whose City? Which Public Interests?" in *Unequal Partnerships: The Political Economy of Urban Redevelopment in Postwar America,* ed. Gregory D. Squires (New Brunswick, NJ: Rutgers University Press), 80–102.

12. Throughout the book, I refer to neighborhood "upgrading" or "incumbent upgrading." These terms refer to Philip Clay's differentiation between improvements made to inspire "gentrification"—the middle-class's rediscovery of inner cities—or those caused by that process, and improvements made through the upgrading of the incumbent population. See Philip L. Clay, *Neighborhood Renewal: Middle-Class Resettlement and Incumbent Upgrading in American Neighborhoods* (Lexington, MA: Lexington Books, 1979). For a current discussion of the lack of this type of analysis in contemporary planning and economic literature, see Ingrid Gould Ellen and Katherine M. O'Regan, "How Low Income Neighborhoods Change: Entry, Exit and Enhancement," *Regional Science and Urban Economics* 41, no. 2 (2011): 89–97.

13. Susan S. Fainstein, *The City Builders: Property Development in New York and London, 1980–2000* (Lawrence: University Press of Kansas, 2001).

14. David Wilson, *Cities and Race: America's New Black Ghetto* (London: Routledge, 2007).

15. Lynne B. Sagalyn, *Times Square Roulette: Remaking the City Icon* (Cambridge, MA: MIT Press, 2001).

16. Lance Freeman, *There Goes the 'Hood: Views of Gentrification from the Ground Up* (Philadelphia: Temple University Press, 2006). One year earlier, Freeman had published a far more controversial piece: "Displacement or Succession? Residential Mobility in Gentrifying Neighborhoods," *Urban Affairs Review* 40, no. 4 (2005): 463–491.

17. Rodin, "The 21st Century Urban University." Ira Harkavy, who is cited throughout the book, has written prolifically on the work he and his colleagues at Penn have been involved in for the past thirty years or more. For a representative work that is critical of the promise of university work in urban communities, see Howell Baum, "Fantasies and Realities in University–Community Partnerships," *Journal of Planning Education and Research* 20, no. 2 (2000): 234–246.

18. James Q. Wilson, "Planning and Politics: Citizen Participation in Urban Renewal," in *Urban Renewal: The Record and the Controversy,* ed. J. Q. Wilson (Cambridge, MA: MIT Press, 1966), 407–421.

19. Grogan and Proscio, *Comeback Cities.* In their introduction, Grogan and Proscio suggest that neighborhood revitalization should not attempt to address the structural sources of poverty, as this goal is largely "irrelevant."

They also dismiss the potential of government policy to alleviate poverty, citing past policy failures as evidence.

20. Rachel Weber, "Extracting Value from the City: Neoliberalism and Urban Development," *Antipode* 34, no. 3 (2002): 519–540.

21. J. J. Stukel, "The Urban University Attacks Real Urban Issues," *Government Finance Review* 10, no. 5 (1994): 19–21.

22. Thomas Bender, *The University and the City: From Medieval Origins to Present* (New York: Oxford University Press, 1988).

23. Thomas Muller, *Immigrants and the American City* (New York: New York University Press, 1993).

24. There are various examples of calls for increased university engagement in the affairs of marginalized urban neighborhoods. Some are for universities to leverage their good deeds for political capital that is needed for things such as campus expansion projects (See Richard M. Freeland, "Universities and Cities Need to Rethink Their Relationships," *Chronicle of Higher Education*, May 13, 2005, B20. Other writings suggest that the commitments universities make to urban neighborhoods should contribute to social justice and the promotion of democratic values. One example of this perspective is Ira Harkavy and John Puckett, "Universities and the Inner Cities," *Planning for Higher Education* 20, no. 4 (1992): 27–32.

25. This is a vast and broad literature. One recent example of an argument for the role of universities in broad regional urban economic development is Richard Florida, "Place-Making after 9/11," in *Cities and the Creative Class* (New York: Routledge, 2005). See also David J. Maurasse, *Beyond the Campus: How Colleges and Universities Form Partnerships with Their Communities* (New York: Routledge, 2001); and Victor Rubin, "The Roles of Universities in Community-Building Initiatives," *Journal of Planning Education and Research* 17, no. 4 (1998): 302–311.

26. Ira Harkavy and H. Zuckerman, "Eds and Meds: Cities' Hidden Assets," (Brookings Institution) *Survey Series*, August 1999, 1–6; see also Carolyn Adams, "The Meds and Eds in Urban Economic Development," *Journal of Urban Affairs* 25, no. 5 (2003): 571–588.

27. Adams, "The Meds and Eds"; Harkavy and Zuckerman, "Eds and Meds."

28. Critiques of the higher education sector and its relative detachment from societal problems or lack of accountability reached new heights after publication of the National Commission on Excellence in Education, *A Nation at Risk: The Imperative for Educational Reform* (Washington, DC: Government Printing Office, 1983). For discussions of the response of higher education to the criticisms outlined in *A Nation at Risk*, see Ernest A. Lynton and Sandra E. Elman, *The New Priorities for the University* (San Francisco: Jossey-Bass, 1987). For a more recent discussion of how one strand

of possible responses implicates a commitment to urban revitalization, consult Ira Harkavy, "The Demands of the Times and the American Research University," *Journal of Planning Literature* 11, no 3 (1997): 333–336.

29. John M. Quigley and Steven Raphael, "Is Housing Unaffordable? Why Isn't It More Affordable?" *Journal of Economic Perspectives* 18, no. 1 (2004): 191–214.

30. This discussion is somewhat undeveloped in the planning literature. Beauregard makes an argument for the antiurban disposition of policy in *Voices of Decline* but stops short of indicting the field of planning at large. Robert Lake makes an argument for this in the closely affiliated field of urban geography in his piece, "The 'Antiurban' Angst of Urban Geography in the 1980s," *Urban Geography* 24, no. 4 (2003): 352–355.

31. Andrew Delbanco, "Scandals of Higher Education," *New York Review of Books*, March 29, 2007, available at http://www.nybooks.com/articles/archives/2007/mar/29/scandals-of-higher-education/?page=1.

32. Manuel Castells, "The Informational City is a Dual City: Can It Be Reversed?" in *High Technology and Low-Income Communities: Prospects for the Positive Use of Advanced Information Technology*, ed. Donald A. Schon, Bish Sanyal, and William Mitchell (Cambridge: MIT Press, 1999), 25–41; and Brian J. Godfrey, "Tragedy and Transformation in New York City," *Geographical Review* 92, no. 1 (January 2002): 127–139.

33. For a more detailed discussion of racial and class exclusion in restructured postindustrial cities, see Loïc J. D. Wacquant and William Julius Wilson, "The Cost of Racial and Class Exclusion in the Inner City," *Annals of the American Academy of Political and Social Science* 501 (January 1989): 8–25.

CHAPTER 2

1. Thomas J. Gibbons, Jr., and Nita Lelyveld, "A Halloween Homicide Jolts a Reeling Penn: Chemist Vladimir Sled Tried to Stop a Purse-Snatching and Was Stabbed 5 Times," *Philadelphia Inquirer*, November 2, 1996, A1.

2. Andrea Ahles, "Shooting, Recent Crimes Spark Outrage among Administrators," *Daily Pennsylvanian*, September 26, 1996, http://www.dailypennsylvanian.com/node/8245.

3. Rodin, "The 21st Century Urban University: New Roles for Practice and Research," *Journal of the American Planning Association* 71, no. 3 (2005): 237–249. See also Judith Rodin, *The University and Urban Revival: Out of the Ivory Tower and into the Streets* (Philadelphia: University of Pennsylvania Press, 2007).

4. "The Rodin Years," *Pennsylvania Gazette*, May–June 2007, 33–41.

5. All university literature and historical documents indicate that Benjamin Franklin wrote his treatise on the education of Pennsylvania's

youth in 1749 and chartered the institution in that year. It took several years for Franklin's academy to secure a location and ultimately hold its first classes, which it did in 1756. This point is not lost on Princeton University historians, who suggest that Penn is the eighth oldest institution of higher learning in the United States, not the fifth. Such a challenge to Penn's founding date is but one of the many to its integrity and reputation that the university has experienced since its founding.

6. Philadelphia was founded by Quakers, whose religious services required no ministers; therefore, there was no need for an institution for clerical training. Franklin's Academy was established for economic and practical reasons. For more detail see George E. Thomas, *The Campus Guide: University of Pennsylvania* (New York: Princeton Architectural Press, 2002).

7. John G. Terino, Jr., "In the Shadow of Spreading Ivy: Science, Culture and the Cold War at the University of Pennsylvania, 1950–1970" (Ph.D. diss., University of Pennsylvania, 2001).

8. Ibid.

9. Ibid.

10. Ibid.

11. Ibid.

12. George E. Thomas and David Brownlee, *Building America's First University: An Historical and Architectural Guide to the University of Pennsylvania* (Philadelphia: University of Pennsylvania Press, 2000), 39; University of Pennsylvania, "University History: Penn Campuses before 1900," Penn University Archives and Records Center, available at http://www.archives .upenn.edu/histy/features/campuses/tour.html.

13. Ibid. Also see Margaret Pugh O'Mara, "Building Brainsville: The University of Pennsylvania and Philadelphia," in *Cities of Knowledge: Cold War Science and the Search for the Next Silicon Valley* (Princeton, NJ: Princeton University Press, 2005); and Charles M. Vest, *Pursuing the Endless Frontier: Essays on MIT and the Role of Research Universities* (Cambridge, MA: MIT Press, 2004).

14. Albert Hirschman, *Exit, Voice, and Loyalty: Responses to Decline in Firms, Organizations, and States* (Cambridge, MA: Harvard University Press, 1970); John Kromer and Lucy Kerman, *West Philadelphia Initiatives: A Case Study in Urban Revitalization* (Philadelphia: University of Pennsylvania Press, 2005).

15. University of Pennsylvania, "The Radian: Project Overview," Penn Connects, http://www.pennconnects.upenn.edu/find_a_project/completed/ completed_2008/the_radian_overview.php.

16. Rachel Baye, "Last Store Standing: The Restaurant Has Sparked Controversy among Administrators and Community Members over the Years," *Daily Pennsylvanian*, February 28, 2011, http://thedp.com/index .php/article/2011/02/last_store_standing_the_past_and_present_of_mcdon alds_at_40th_and_walnut.

17. See University of Pennsylvania, "Appendix III: Digest of Valley Forge Plan," board of trustees meeting minutes, May 22, 1936, available at http://www.archives.upenn.edu/primdocs/uplan/valforgemay1936.pdf; also see Rodin, "The 21st Century Urban University."

18. Rodin, *The University and Urban Revival*, 24.

19. For a full description of the Penn Compact, see http://www.upenn .edu/compact.

20. Princeton, originally known as the College of New Jersey, was first located in Newark, New Jersey, then in Elizabeth, and finally in Princeton. Columbia, originally known as King's College, moved from its first location in Lower Manhattan, then to two different midtown Manhattan locations, and finally to its current location in Morningside Heights/Harlem.

21. The university's alumni magazine, the *Pennsylvania Gazette*, has run several stories about Gutmann and her inaugural. In them, Gutmann outlines her decision to be considered for and to accept the position at Penn. She also discusses the confluence between her intellectual work and her plans for her tenure. See John Prendergast, "Learning and Leading," *Pennsylvania Gazette* 103, no. 1 (September–October 2004): 30–37; and "A Marriage Meant to Be: Amy Gutmann Inaugurated as Penn's Eighth President," *Pennsylvania Gazette* 103, no. 2 (2004): 30–41. The latter issue also contains the text of her inaugural address and a report on the symposium that followed. Amy Gutmann has written extensively on the topics of difference, critical democracy, and democracy in education. Her work includes *Democratic Education* (with Kwame Appiah) (Princeton, NJ: Princeton University Press, 1987); *Color Conscious: The Political Morality of Race* (Princeton, NJ: Princeton University Press, 1996); *Democracy and Disagreement* (with Dennis Thompson) (Cambridge, MA: Belknap Press, 1996); *Identity in Democracy* (Princeton, NJ: Princeton University Press, 2003); and *Why Deliberative Democracy* (with Dennis Thompson) (Princeton, NJ: Princeton University Press, 2004).

22. See O'Mara, "Building Brainsville"; and Terino, "In the Shadow of Spreading Ivy."

23. See the publications of noted sociologist William Foote Whyte, who authored such works as *Street Corner Society: The Social Structure of an Italian Slum* (Chicago: University of Chicago Press, 1943).

24. Derek Bok, *Universities and the Future of America* (Durham, NC: Duke University Press, 1990); Davydd Greenwood and Morton Levin, "Reconstructing the Relationships between Universities and Society through Action Research," in *Handbook of Qualitative Research: Strategies for Qualitative Inquiry*, 2nd ed., ed. Norman K. Denzin and Yvonne S. Lincoln (Thousand Oaks, CA: Sage, 2003); Clark Kerr, *The Uses of the University*, 5th ed. (Cambridge, MA: Harvard University Press, 2001); Christopher Newfield, *Ivy and Industry: Business and the Making of the American University,*

1880–1980 (Durham, NC: Duke University Press, 2003); and S. Slaughter and L. Leslie, *Academic Capitalism: Politics, Policies and the Entrepreneurial University* (Baltimore: Johns Hopkins University Press, 1997).

25. Harley Etienne, "University/Community Relations: Public Rhetoric and Private Interests" (master's thesis, Temple University, 2001).

26. Ira Harkavy and John Puckett, "The Role of Mediating Structures in University and Community Revitalization: The University of Pennsylvania and West Philadelphia as a Case Study," *Journal of Research and Development in Education* 25, no. 1 (Fall 1991): 10–25.

27. At some point between Hackney's creation of OCOPS and Rodin's arrival, OCOPS was transformed into the Penn Center for Public Service (PCPS). The reporting structure between it and the president remained intact. The change from OCOPS to PCPS reflected the growing stature and importance of service-learning courses to the community engagement strategy.

28. The Wharton School operates the Small Business Development Center, which provides technical assistance and counseling to small business owners of all kinds.

29. Trymaine Lee, "Bracing for the Lion," *New York Times*, July 22, 2007.

30. Terino, "In the Shadow of Spreading Ivy."

CHAPTER 3

1. Judith Rodin, "The Inaugural Address," *(University of Pennsylvania) Almanac* 41, no. 9 (October 25, 1994): S-4–S-7, available at http://www.upenn.edu/almanac/v41pdf/n09/102594-insert.pdf.

2. Lynn Lees, Walter Licht, and Richard Shell, "Speaking Out: Neighborhood and Urban Agenda," *Penn Almanac* 43, no. 9 (1996), available at http://www.upenn.edu/almanac/v43/n09/spouturb.html.

3. John Kromer and Lucy Kerman, *West Philadelphia Initiatives: A Case Study in Urban Revitalization* (Philadelphia: University of Pennsylvania Press, 2005).

4. Figures calculated by the author using data from the parcelBase, City of Philadelphia Bureau of Revision and Taxes/Cartographic Modeling Laboratory, University of Pennsylvania, June 2006.

5. Kromer and Kerman, *West Philadelphia Initiatives*, 34.

6. The term "bougie" is a euphemism for "bourgeois" that is intended to insult.

7. For a detailed chronology of the Pennsylvania state government takeover of the School District of Philadelphia, see Eva Travers, "Philadelphia School Reform: Historical Roots and Reflections on the 2002–2003 School Year under State Takeover," *Penn GSE Perspectives on Urban Education* 2, no. 2 (Fall 2003), available at http://www.urbanedjournal.org/archive/Issue4/commentaries/comment0007.html.

8. For a further discussion of how schools are used to market and revitalize urban neighborhoods, see David P. Varady and Jeffrey A. Raffel, *Selling Cities: Attracting Homebuyers through Schools and Housing Programs* (Albany: State University of New York Press, 1995).

9. Richard D. Taub, Garth Taylor, and Jan D. Dunham, *Paths of Neighborhood Change: Race and Crime in Urban America* (Chicago: University of Chicago Press, 1984).

10. Ibid., 182.

11. William N. Evans and Emily Owens, "COPS and Crime," *Journal of Public Economics* 91, no. 1–2 (February): 181–201.

12. Federal Bureau of Investigation, *Crime in the United States, 2005* (Washington, DC: U.S. Department of Justice, Federal Bureau of Investigation, 2006), available at http://www2.fbi.gov/ucr/05cius/.

13. Ibid., table 8, available at http://www2.fbi.gov/ucr/05cius/data/table_08_pa.html.

14. Data from the City of Philadelphia Police Department via crimeBase, Cartographic Modeling Laboratory, University of Pennsylvania.

15. See University City District, *University City Report Card 2007* (Philadelphia: University City District, 2007), p. 30 for a full description of the "yellow shirt" security patrol sponsored by the business improvement district.

16. Lance Freeman, *There Goes the 'Hood: Views of Gentrification from the Ground Up* (Philadelphia: Temple University Press, 2006).

17. This analysis was conducted using decennial census data and American Community Survey data from 1990 and 2000 and five-year-estimate data from 2005 to 2009 for census tracts 76, 77, 79, 86, 87, 88, 89, 90, 91, and 92, which approximate the area defined as University City by the University City District and the University of Pennsylvania's Penn Home Ownership Services Office. For complete data, see http://www.socialexplorer.com/pub/blog/?p=1469.

18. Thomas Sugrue, *The Origins of the Urban Crisis: Post War Detroit*, 2nd ed. (Princeton, NJ: Princeton University Press, 2005).

19. University City District, *University City Report Card 2007* (Philadelphia: University City District, 2007, p. 8.

20. University of Pennsylvania, *Penn Economic Impact Report, FY 2010*, available at http://www.evp.upenn.edu/docs/PennEconomicImpact_SlideShow.pdf.

21. Gerry Riposa, "From Enterprise Zones to Empowerment Zones," *American Behavioral Scientist* 39, no. 5 (1996): 536–551; U.S. Department of Housing and Urban Development, *Building Communities Together* (Washington, DC: Government Printing Office, 1994); U.S. Department of Housing and Urban Development, *Urban Empowerment Zones and Enterprise Communities* (HUD-1551-CPD, Washington, DC: Government Printing Office, 1995).

22. Herbert Lowe, "'Jump Street' Gets the Spotlight: Local Leaders Formally Announced the Development; They Expect Big Things for North Broad Street," *Philadelphia Inquirer*, July 7, 1998, B1.

23. Inga Saffron, "Welcome back, Girard Avenue: A Street Reborn; Girard Avenue Revival," *Philadelphia Inquirer*, January 9, 2004, E1.

24. City of Philadelphia, "Neighborhood Transformation Initiative Progress Report, 2000–2003: Transforming Our Neighborhoods—Building Our Future" (report of the Philadelphia City Planning Commission, 2003); Lisa K. Bates, *A Housing Submarket Approach to Neighborhood Planning: Theoretical Considerations and Empirical Justifications* (Ph.D. diss., University of North Carolina, Chapel Hill, 2003); "Market Value Analysis: Philadelphia," Reinvestment Fund, 2006, http://www.trfund.com/planning/market-phila .html.

25. The Reinvestment Fund (TRF) has continually updated its analysis in order to gauge the program's effectiveness. In 2001, the "University City West" area (as defined by this study) was considered to be a mix of "stressed" and "transitional." In 2003, it was upgraded to "steady," while portions of "University City Central" that overlapped with the Penn-Alexander School catchments area were upgraded to "regional choice" by TRF's analysis.

26. Stephen J. McGovern, "Philadelphia's Neighborhood Transformation Initiative: A Case Study of Mayoral Leadership, Bold Planning, and Conflict," *Housing Policy Debate* 17, no. 3 (2006): 529–570.

27. Paul Nussbaum, "SEPTA Celebrates End of Market Street El Work," *Philadelphia Inquirer*, September 12, 2009, B2.

CHAPTER 4

1. In his article on political language, Murray Edelman presents an argument that shows how political language can complicate our understandings of political realities. I am implicitly employing his logic to support the claim that the term "revitalization" at one time suggested more about "incumbent upgrading" and not "social mobility" or gentrification. See Murray Edelman, "Political Language and Political Reality," *PS* 80, no. 1(1985):10–19. Also see Philip Clay, *Neighborhood Renewal: Middle-Class Resettlement and Incumbent Upgrading in American Neighborhoods* (Lexington, MA: Lexington Books, 1979), for a discussion of two distinct modes of neighborhood revitalization.

2. Dennis E. Gale, *Neighborhood Revitalization and the Postindustrial City* (Lexington, MA: Lexington Books, 1984).

3. Elijah Anderson, *Streetwise: Race, Class and Change in an Urban Community* (Chicago: University of Chicago Press, 1990); Brett Williams, *Upscaling Downtown: Stalled Gentrification in Washington, D.C.* (Ithaca, NY: Cornell University Press, 1988); William Julius Wilson and Richard P. Taub,

There Goes the Neighborhood: Racial, Ethnic and Class Tensions in Four Chicago Neighborhoods and Their Meaning for America (New York: Alfred A. Knopf, 2006).

4. Gale, *Neighborhood Revitalization and the Postindustrial City.* See also W. Dennis Keating, "Introduction: Neighborhoods in Urban America," in *Revitalizing Urban Neighborhoods,* ed. W. Dennis Keating, Norman Krumholz, and Philip Star, 1–6 (Lawrence: University Press of Kansas, 1996); Susan S. Fainstein, *City Builders: Property Development in New York and London, 1980– 2000,* 2nd ed. (Lawrence: University Press of Kansas, 2000); Jason Hackworth, *The Neoliberal City: Governance, Ideology, and Development in American Urbanism* (Ithaca, NY: Cornell University Press, 2007).

5. Paul S. Grogan and Tony Proscio, *Comeback Cities: A Blueprint for Urban Neighborhood Revival* (Boulder, CO: Westview Press, 2000).

6. One critique of the works of Anderson, Wilson and Taub, and, to a lesser extent, Williams is that they disguise their subjects for the purposes of confidentiality. The consequence is a lack of situational context and specificity. Although Anderson and Wilson and Taub provide some descriptive statistics, further detail about the specific roles institutions play in neighborhood change would have been useful.

7. Richard Taub, D. Garth Taylor, and Jan D. Dunham, *Paths of Neighborhood Change: Race and Crime in Urban America* (Chicago: University of Chicago Press, 1984).

8. Lincoln Quillian and Devah Pager, "Black Neighbors, Higher Crime? The Role of Racial Stereotypes in Evaluations of Neighborhood Crime," *American Journal of Sociology*107, no. 3 (2001): 717–763.

9. Lance Freeman, "Displacement or Succession? Residential Mobility in Gentrifying Neighborhoods," *Urban Affairs Review* 40, no. 4 (2005): 463–491.

10. Carol B. Stack, *All Our Kin: Strategies for Survival in a Black Community* (New York: Harper and Row, 1974); Katherine S. Newman, *No Shame in My Game: The Working Poor in the Inner City* (New York: Alfred A. Knopf and the Russell Sage Foundation, 1974).

11. Howell S. Baum, "Smart Growth and School Reform: What If We Talked about Race and Took Community Seriously?" *Journal of the American Planning Association* 70, no. 1 (2004): 14–26.

12. Kent P. Schwirian, "Models of Neighborhood Change," *Annual Review of Sociology* 9 (1983): 83–102; S. Keller, *The Urban Neighborhood* (New York: Random House, 1968).

13. Schwirian, "Models of Neighborhood Change," 84.

14. Emily Talen, "The Problem with Community," *Journal of Planning Literature* 15 (2000): 171–183.

15. Mary Pattillo-McCoy "The Limits of Out-Migration for the Black Middle Class, *Journal of Urban Affairs* 22, no. 3 (Fall 2000): 225–241.

16. David Harvey, "The New Urbanism and the Communitarian Trap: On Social Problems and the False Hope of Design," *Harvard Design Magazine,* no. 1 (Winter/Spring 1997): 1–3.

17. J. John Palen and Bruce London, eds. *Gentrification, Displacement and Neighborhood Revitalization* (Albany: State University of New York Press, 1984). An updated categorization might include a substantial subcategory of megaprojects within the political-economic framework, if not a separate subcategory altogether. This is important because I understand Penn's work in West Philadelphia to be a form of megaproject or at least a comprehensive planning project.

18. See Roderick D. McKenzie, "The Ecological Approach to the Study of Human Community," in *The City,* ed. Robert Park (with Ernest Burgess, Roderick McKenzie, and Louis Wirth) (Chicago: University of Chicago Press, 1925): 287–301; Robert A. Park, *Human Communities* (Glencoe, IL: Free Press, 1952); E. M. Hoover and R. Vernon, *Anatomy of a Metropolis* (Cambridge, MA: Harvard University Press, 1959); Schwirian, "Models of Neighborhood Change," 90.

19. Robert E. Park (with Ernest W. Burgess, Roderick McKenzie, and Louis Wirth), *The City* (Chicago: University of Chicago Press, 1925); O. D. Duncan and B. Duncan, *The Negro Population in Chicago* (Chicago: University of Chicago Press, 1957).

20. Elijah Anderson, introduction to *The Philadelphia Negro,* by W.E.B. DuBois (Philadelphia: University of Pennsylvania Press, 1996).

21. Ibid., xv.

22. Susan S. Fainstein and Norman I. Fainstein, introduction to *Restructuring the City: The Political Economy of Urban Redevelopment,* by Susan Fainstein, Norman I. Fainstein, Richard Child Hill, Dennis Judd, and Michael P. Smith (New York: Longman, 1986); David Harvey, *The Urbanization of Capital: Studies in the History and Theory of Capitalist Urbanization* (Baltimore: Johns Hopkins University Press, 1985).

23. Susan Fainstein and Mia Gray, "Economic Development Strategies for the Inner City: The Need for Governmental Intervention," in *The Inner City: Urban Poverty and Economic Development in the Next Century,* ed. Thomas D. Boston and Catherine L. Ross, (New Brunswick, NJ: Transaction Publishers, 1997).

24. Many studies document the history of urban decline in American cities. Three excellent examples stand out, each written in a different era and covering a different city, and yet all reaching similar conclusions. They are W.E.B. DuBois, *The Philadelphia Negro: A Social Study* (Philadelphia: University of Pennsylvania Press, 1996); Arnold R. Hirsch, *Making the Second Ghetto: Race and Housing in Chicago, 1940–1960* (Chicago: University of Chicago Press,

1998); and Thomas Sugrue, *The Origins of the Urban Crisis: Race and Inequality in Postwar Detroit* (Princeton, NJ: Princeton University Press, 2005).

25. Peter Dreier, "American's Urban Crisis: Symptoms, Causes and Solutions," in *Race, Poverty and American Cities*, ed. John Charles Boger with Judith Welch Wegner (Chapel Hill: University of North Carolina Press, 1993), 81.

26. Douglas S. Massey and Nancy A. Denton, *American Apartheid: Segregation and the Making of the Underclass* (Cambridge, MA: Harvard University Press, 1993).

27. Michael B. Teitz and Karen Chapple, "The Causes of Inner-City Poverty: Eight Hypotheses in Search of Reality," *Cityscape: A Journal of Policy Development and Research* 3, no. 3 (1998): 33–70.

28. Harvey, *The Urbanization of Capital*.

29. Neil Smith, *The New Urban Frontier: Gentrification and the Revanchist City* (London: Routledge, 1996).

30. Smith, *The New Urban Frontier*; John J. Palen and Bruce London, eds., *Gentrification, Displacement and Neighborhood Revitalization* (Albany: SUNY Press, 1984); Tom Slater, "The Eviction of Critical Perspectives from Gentrification Research," *International Journal of Urban and Regional Research* 30, no. 4 (2006): 737–757.

31. Loretta Lees, Tom Slater, and Elvin K. Wyly, *Gentrification* (London: Routledge, 2008).

32. Tom Slater, "The Eviction of Critical Perspectives from Gentrification Research."

33. Hackworth, *The Neoliberal City*, 126–128.

34. Scott Campbell and Susan S. Fainstein, "Introduction: The Structure and Debates of Planning Theory," in *Readings in Planning Theory*, 2nd ed., ed. Scott Campbell and Susan S. Fainstein (London: Blackwell, 2003), 1–16.

35. Richard E. Klosterman, "Arguments for and against Planning," *Town Planning Review* 56, no. 1 (1985): 5–20.

36. David Harvey, "On Planning the Ideology of Planning," in *The Urbanization of Capital* (Baltimore: Johns Hopkins University Press, 1985), 165–184; Neil Smith, *Uneven Development: Nature, Capital, and the Production of Space* (Athens: University of Georgia Press, 2008).

37. Bernard Frieden and Lynn Sagalyn, *Downtown, Inc.: How America Rebuilds Cities* (Cambridge, MA: MIT Press, 1989).

38. Thomas Sugrue, "Revisiting the Second Ghetto," *Journal of Urban History* 29 (2003): 281.

39. Arnold R. Hirsch, *Making the Second Ghetto: Race and Housing in Chicago, 1940–1960* (Chicag: University of Chicago Press, 1998), 135–170; also see Margaret Pugh O'Mara, *Cities of Knowledge: Cold War Science and the Search for the Next Silicon Valley* (Princeton, NJ: Princeton University Press, 2005).

40. See Philip Kasinitz, "Bringing the Neighborhood Back In: The New Urban Ethnography," *Sociological Forum* 7, no. 2 (1992): 355–363; and Paul Willis, *Learning to Labor: How Working Class Kids Get Working Class Jobs* (New York: Columbia University Press, 1982).

41. Hirsch, *Making the Second Ghetto*; O'Mara, *Cities of Knowledge*.

42. John Forester, "Conservative Epistemology, Reductive Ethics, Far Too Narrow Politics: Some Clarifications in Response to Yiftacheland Huxley," *International Journal of Urban and Regional Research* 2, no. 4 (2000): 914–916.

43. Susan Christopherson and Jennifer Clark, *Remaking Regional Economies: Power, Labor and Firm Strategies in the Knowledge Economy* (New York: Routledge, 2009).

44. Manuel Castells, "The Informational City Is a Dual City: Can It Be Reversed?" in *High Technology and Low-Income Communities: Prospects for the Positive Use of Advanced Information Technology*, ed. Donald A. Schon, Bish Sanyal, and William Mitchell (Cambridge: MIT Press, 1999), 31. Italics in original.

45. Fainstein, *The City Builders*.

CHAPTER 5

1. Dobelle's criteria include length of involvement with the community; real dollars invested; catalyst effect on others; presence felt through payroll, research, and purchasing power; faculty and student involvement in community service; continued sustainability of neighborhood initiatives; effect on local student access and affordability of college through K–12 partnerships; qualitative esprit of the institution in its engagement; quantifiable increase in positive recognition of the institution; increase in student applications and resources raised through renewed alumni giving; and recognition of the impact of these institutions within their community. For more, see Evan S. Dobelle, "Saviors of Our Cities: 2009 Survey of College and University Civic Partnerships," Fall 2009, available at http://www.evandobelle.com/SOOC%20Survey%20Overview.pdf.

2. Audrey Williams June, "As It Seeks More Room, Columbia Treads Carefully: A Planned $5-Billion Development in Neighboring Harlem Reawakens Old Animosities," *Chronicle of Higher Education*, October 1, 2004, A29.

3. For more on Columbia's Manhattanville plans, see http://www.neighbors.columbia.edu/pages/manplanning/index.html.

4. William Richards, "Architecture's Communards at Columbia" (paper, Annual Meetings of the *Association of American Geographers*, Washington, DC, April 15, 2010). See also Peter Marcuse and Cuz Potter, "Columbia University's Heights: An Ivory Tower and Its Communities," in *The University as Urban Developer: Case Studies and Analysis*, ed. David C. Perry and Wim

Wiewel (Armonk, NY: M. E. Sharpe, 2005), 45–64; David J. Craig, "Smart Growth: Columbia's Got a Long Range Plan to Advance Academic and Revitalize West Harlem," *Columbia Magazine*, June 2006, 8–15, available at http://www.neighbors.columbia.edu/pages/manplanning/pdf-files/colum bia_mag_june06.pdf.

5. Marcuse and Potter, "Columbia University's Heights."

6. Allegra Calder, Gabrial Grant, and Holly Hart Muson, "No Such Thing as Vacant Land: Northeastern University and Davenport Commons," in *The University as Urban Developer: Case Studies and Analysis*, ed. David C. Perry and Wim Wiewel (Armonk, NY: M. E. Sharpe, 2005), 253–267.

7. Deborah Kelnotic, "Building a New Northeastern: The West Campus Residence Hall Opens an Era," *Northeastern University Magazine*, September 1999, http://www.northeastern.edu/magazine/9909/westcamp.html.

8. Calder, Grant, and Muson, "No Such Thing as Vacant Land," 258.

9. Scott Martindale, "Defining Downtown: USC Boundaries Expanding within Limits," *Daily Trojan*, November 14, 2001, 2–8.

10. Dan Loeterman, "Long-Term Community Residents Oppose USC Master Plan Details" Strategic Actions for a Just Economy, April 3, 2008, http://www.saje.net/site/c.hkLQJcMUKrH/b.3998783/k.D068/ Residents_Oppose_Master_Plan.htm.

11. Wendy Thomas, "Store's Closure a Blow to USC Neighborhood," *Los Angeles Times*, September 30, 2005, http://articles.latimes.com/2005/ sep/30/local/me-market30.

12. For more information about the University of Southern California's planning goals and objectives, see University of Southern California, "University Park Campus Master Planning," available at http://www.usc .edu/community/upcmasterplan; and University of Southern California, "USC Master Plan 2030—Fact Sheet," May 27, 2008, available at http:// www.nandc.org/docs/land_use/USCMstrPlan-FinalMtgDocs.pdf.

13. Allston Development Group (Cooper, Robertson & Partners, Gehry Partners, and Olin Partnership), *The Plan for Harvard in Allston (Draft): Executive Summary* (New York: Cooper, Robertson 2007); Harvard president Drew Gilpin Faust announced in the *Harvard Gazette* that the Allston developments would continue, albeit at a much slower pace because of the global economic crisis that had devalued Harvard's endowment and forced a review of all ongoing projects. For more information, see "Allston Update Letter," *Harvard Gazette*, February 19, 2009, available at http://news.harvard.edu/ gazette/story/2009/02/allston-update-letter.

14. John Lauerman, "Harvard's Purcell to Advise on Expansion in Boston's Allston Neighborhood," *Bloomberg*, April 20, 2010, http://www .bloomberg.com/news/2010-04-20/harvard-s-purcell-to-advise-on-expansion-in-boston-s-allston-neighborhood.html.

15. Gillian Wee, "Harvard to Raise 'Several Hundred Million' from Property Sales," *Bloomberg*, February 17, 2010, http://www.bloomberg.com/apps/news?pid=washingtonstory&sid=aZWJS44lDy4M.

16. Ziona Austrian and Jill S. Norton, "An Overview of University Real Estate Investment Practices," in *The University as Urban Developer: Case Studies and Analysis*, ed. David C. Perry and Wim Wiewel (Armonk, NY: M. E. Sharpe, 2005), 193–221.

CHAPTER 6

1. Universities now offer diverse activities and support services, including transportation networks, health care services, police, university-owned or -managed retail, housing services, and banks.

2. Thomas Sugrue, *The Origins of the Urban Crisis: Race and Inequality in Postwar Detroit* (Princeton, NJ: Princeton University Press, 2005); Bennett Harrison, *Lean and Mean: The Changing Landscape of Corporate Power in the Age of Flexibility* (New York: Basic Books, 1994).

3. Charles E. McClelland, "'To Live for Science': Ideals and Realities at the University of Berlin," in *The University and the City*, ed. T. Bender (Oxford: Oxford University Press, 1988), 181–197; Donald N. Levine, "The Idea of the University, Take One: On the Genius of This Place" (paper, Idea of the University Colloquium, University of Chicago, November 8, 2000).

4. Claudia Goldin and Michael Katz, "The Shaping of Higher Education: The Formative Years in the United States," *Journal of Economic Perspectives* 13, no. 1 (1999): 37–62; Thomas Bender, "Scholarship, Local Life and the Necessity of Worldliness," in *The Urban University and its Identity*, ed. Herman van der Wusten (Dordrecht, Netherlands: Kluwer Academic Publishers, 1998), 17–28.

5. Bender, "Scholarship, Local Life and the Necessity of Worldliness," 7.

6. Herman van der Wusten, ed., *The Urban University and its Identity* (Dordrecht, Netherlands: Kluwer Academic Publishers, 1998).

7. Lee Benson and Ira Harkavy, "Saving the Soul of the University: What Is to Be Done?" in *The Virtual University: Knowledge, Markets and Management*, ed. Kevin Robins and Frank Webster (Oxford: Oxford University Press, 2002), 169–209; George E. Thomas, *The Campus Guide: University of Pennsylvania* (New York: Princeton Architectural Press, 2002).

8. John Terino, "In the Shadow of Spreading Ivy" (Ph.D. diss., University of Pennsylvania, 2001); Thomas, *The Campus Guide.*

9. Thomas Bender, *The University and the City: From Medieval Origins to Present* (New York: Oxford University Press, 1988).

10. David C. Perry and Wim Wiewel, "From Campus to City: The University as Developer," in *The University as Urban Developer: Case Studies and*

Analysis, ed. David C. Perry and Wim Wiewel (Armonk, NY: M. E. Sharpe, 2005), 3–21; Thomas, *The Campus Guide*.

11. Bender, *The University and the City*; John Henry Newman, *The Idea of a University*, ed. Frank M. Turner (New Haven, CT: Yale University Press, 1996). In more contemporary times, the pastoral image of the university campus meshes well with a desire to establish institutions that serve the contemporary middle-class consumer tastes of many students.

12. Sugrue, *The Origins of the Urban Crisis*.

13. Barry Bluestone and Mary Huff Stevenson, *The Boston Renaissance: Race, Space, and Economic Change in an American Metropolis* (New York: Russell Sage Foundation, 2000); Margaret Pugh O'Mara, *Cities of Knowledge* (Princeton, NJ: Princeton University Press, 2005).

14. Claudia Goldin and Michael Katz, "The Shaping of Higher Education: The Formative Years in the United States," *Journal of Economic Perspectives* 13, no 1 (1999): 37–62. In the Victorian period, universities in both Europe and the United States were criticized for "losing touch with reality." Curricular reforms and the founding of new institutions focused on more practical studies and applications of knowledge.

15. Van der Wusten, *The Urban University and Its Identity*; Benson and Harkavy, "Saving the Soul of the University."

16. J. Martin Klotsche, *The Urban University and the Future of Our Cities* (New York: Harper and Row, 1966), 10.

17. Ibid; James Crooks, "The AUU and the Mission of the Urban University," *Urbanism Past and Present* 7, no. 2 (1982): 34–39.

18. Klotsche, *The Urban University and the Future of Our Cities*.

19. The implication here, of course, is that most American colleges were traditionally the preserve of the privileged classes and as a result were contradictory to the demands of a democratic society. For further discussion, see Crooks, "The AUU and the Mission of the Urban University."

20. Bender, "Scholarship, Local Life and the Necessity of Worldliness," 24.

21. Benson and Harkavy, "Saving the Soul of the University."

22. Michael S. Fogarty and Amit K. Sinha, "Why Older Regions Can't Generalize from Route 128 and Silicon Valley: University–Industry Relationships and Regional Innovation Systems," in *Industrializing Knowledge: University–Industry Linkages in Japan and the United States*, ed. Lewis M. Branscomb, Fumio Kodama, and Richard Florida (Cambridge, MA: MIT Press, 1999), 473–509; O'Mara, *Cities of Knowledge*; AnnaLee Saxenian, *Regional Advantage: Culture and Competition in Silicon Valley and Route 128* (Cambridge, MA: Harvard University Press, 1994).

23. Initiative for a Competitive Inner City and CEOs for Cities, *Leveraging Colleges and Universities for Urban Economic Revitalization* (Boston: ICIC, 2002).

24. Clark Kerr, *The Uses of the University*, 5th ed. (Cambridge, MA: Harvard University Press, 2001).

25. Several articles on college and university presidential searches reached mainstream media outlets. In 2007 alone, the *New York Times* published two on high-profile searches at Harvard University and Morehouse College in Atlanta. Both referred to the fact that academic presidential searches have, in spite of their explicit intentions to be confidential and private, become public and highly political processes. In Harvard's case, publicity given to the search caused several candidates to withdraw from further consideration. See Alan Finder, "Headhunters at Harvard May Pick a Woman," *New York Times*, January 8, 2007, available at http://www.nytimes.com/2007/01/08/education/08harvard.html; and Shaila Dewan, "Morehouse Searches for a Leader and a Way to Keep Making Gains," *New York Times*, March 28, 2007, B7.

26. Burton R. Clark, *Creating Entrepreneurial Universities: Organizational Pathways of Transformation* (Paris: IAU Press, 1998), 5.

27. Daniel Nelson, *Frederick W. Taylor and the Rise of Scientific Management* (Madison: University of Wisconsin Press, 1980).

28. See Andrew Delbanco, "Scandals of Higher Education," *New York Review of Books*, March 29, 2007, http://www.nybooks.com/articles/archives/2007/mar/29/scandals-of-higher-education/, for a broader discussion of how elite colleges are becoming even more exclusive through their tuition discounting and amenity development programs. Gene Winter "Jacuzzi U.? A Battle of Perks to Lure Students," *New York Times*, October 5, 2003, 1, available at http://www.nytimes.com/2003/10/05/us/jacuzzi-u-a-battle-of-perks-to-lure-students.html?pagewanted=all&src=pm, speaks more directly to interinstitutional competition for top students through amenities. See also Sue Westcott Alessandri, Sung-Un Yang, and Dennis F. Kensey, "An Integrative Approach to University Visual Identity and Reputation," *Corporate Reputation Review* 9, no. 4 (2006): 258–270, for an account of the extent to which large private universities have come to manage their visual identity, of which their campus and its environs are a part.

29. Cara Baruzzi, "Yale University Drives Downtown Retail Renewal," *New Haven Register*, October 30, 2005, available at http://nhregister.com/articles/2005/10/30/import/15479564.txt.

30. Patrick Ward, "Retail Monopoly Bad for Shoppers, Profits, *Yale Daily News*, March 27, 2007, available at http://www.yaledailynews.com/news/2007/mar/27/retail-monopoly-bad-for-shoppers-profits.

31. Sugrue, *The Origins of the Urban Crisis*.

32. Crooks, "The AUU and the Mission of the Urban University."

33. Paul Davidoff, "Advocacy and Pluralism in Planning," *Journal of the American Institute of Planners* 31 (November 1965): 331–338; Lisa R. Peattie,

"Reflections in Advocacy Planning," *Journal of the American Institute of Planners* 34, no. 2 (1968): 80–87.

34. June Manning Thomas, *Redevelopment and Race* (Baltimore: Johns Hopkins University Press, 1997); James Q. Wilson, "Planning and Politics: Citizen Participation in Urban Renewal," in *Urban Renewal: The Record and the Controversy*, ed. James Q. Wilson (Cambridge, MA: MIT Press, 1966), 407–421.

35. Terino, "In the Shadow of Spreading Ivy"; Klotsche, *The Urban University and the Future of our Cities*; Jon C. Teaford, *The Rough Road to Renaissance: Urban Revitalization in America, 1940–1985* (Baltimore: Johns Hopkins University Press, 1990); M. Gordon Seyffert, "The University as Urban Neighbor," in *Universities in the Urban Crisis*, ed. T. P. Murphy (New York: Dunellen Publishing Company, 1975), 137–159.

36. Crooks, "The AUU and the Mission of the Urban University."

37. Ira Harkavy and John Puckett, "The Role of Mediating Structures in University and Community Revitalization: The University of Pennsylvania and West Philadelphia as a Case Study," *Journal of Research and Development in Education* 25, no. 1 (1991): 10–25; Benson and Harkavy, "Saving the Soul of the University"; David J. Maurasse, *Beyond the Campus: How Colleges and Universities Form Partnerships with Their Communities* (New York: Routledge, 2001).

38. Vicky Carweign, Sandra Boyle, John Idstrom, and Mike Wark, "Capitalizing on Community: Turning Community Relations into the Biggest Asset of a New Campus," *Metropolitan Universities* 12, no. 2 (2001): 68–76.

39. Howell S. Baum, "Fantasies and Realities in University–Community Partnerships," *Journal of Planning Education and Research* 20 (2000): 234–246; Jean B. Tyler and Martin Maberman, "Education–Community Partnerships: Who Uses Whom and for What Purposes?" *Metropolitan Universities* 13, no. 4 (2002): 88–100.

40. Baum, "Fantasies and Realities in University–Community Partnerships."

41. O'Mara, *Cities of Knowledge*; Bluestone and Stevenson, *The Boston Renaissance*; Saxenian, *Regional Advantage*; Richard Florida and Wesley M. Cohen, "Engine or Infrastructure? The University Role in Economic Development." In *Industrializing Knowledge: University–Industry Linkages in Japan and the United States*, ed. Lewis M. Branscomb, Fumio Kodama, and Richard Florida (Cambridge, MA: MIT Press, 1999), 589–610; and Fumio Kodama and Lewis M. Branscomb, "University Research as an Engine for Growth: How Realistic Is the Vision?" in *Industrializing Knowledge: University–Industry Links in Japan and the United States*, ed. Lewis M. Branscomb, Fumio Kodama, and Richard Florida (Cambridge: MIT Press, 1999), 3–19.

42. Daniel Felsenstein, "The University in the Metropolitan Arena: Impacts and Public Policy Implications," *Urban Studies* 33, no. 9 (1996): 1565–1580; Harvey A. Goldstein and Catherine S. Renault, "Contributions of Universities to Regional Economic Development: A Quasi-Experimental Approach," *Regional Studies* 38, no. 7 (2004): 733–746.

43. Benson and Harkavy, "Saving the Soul of the University."

44. Richard Florida, *Cities and the Creative Class* (New York: Routledge, 2005).

45. University and Small Business Patent Procedures Act. 35 U.S.C. §200–212 (1980).

46. In recent years, a number of universities, particularly elite research-extensive universities, have issued "economic impact reports" to show how valuable they are as drivers of economic growth. Some common themes in these reports are contributions to the labor market through hiring, direct and indirect spending, and income earned by local alumni.

47. Universities that receive annual allocations tend to focus their attention on their impacts on local economies and markets, whereas others, such as the University of Pennsylvania, balance that focus with a focus on statewide and super-regional impacts. For a quick comparison, see Cornell University's report at http://landgrant.cornell.edu/cu/cms/landgrant/impact/upload/econ-impact-2009.pdf and a summary of the 2010 *Penn Economic Impact Report* at http://www.evp.upenn.edu/docs/PennEconomicImpact_SlideShow.pdf.

48. Irwin Feller, "S & T-Based Economic Development and the University: Virtuous and Vicious Cycles in the Contributions of Public Research Universities to State Economic Development Objectives," *Economic Development Quarterly* 18, no. 2 (2004):138–150.

49. Michael VerMeulen, "The University as Landlord." *Institutional Investor* 14, no. 5 (1980): 119–122.

50. Ibid.

51. The literature on antiurban biases is far too broad to attribute to one source. From Upton Sinclair's *The Jungle* to works cited elsewhere in this book, such as Thomas Sugrue's *Origins of the Urban Crisis*, it is clear that American culture has long associated urban life with crime, poverty, deprivation, and, largely, the plight of poor African Americans. Although antiurban bias in the United States can trace its roots to the religious leaders who established the colonies and to anti-urban bias in Europe, it is fair to say that a relationship exists between the establishment of many American colleges and universities, their host locations and relationships to them, campus planning practices and design standards, and an anti-urban bias.

52. Clark Kerr, *The Uses of the University*, 5th ed. (Cambridge, MA: Harvard University Press, 2001).

53. Audrey Williams June, "As It Seeks More Room, Columbia Treads Carefully: A Planned $5-Billion Development in Neighboring Harlem Reawakens Old Animosities." *Chronicle of Higher Education*, October 1, 2004, A29.

54. Perry and Wiewel, "From Campus to City."

55. Davydd J. Greenwood, "Who Are the Real 'Problem Owners'? On the Social Embeddedness of Universities," in *Bright Satanic Mills: Universities, Regional Development and the Knowledge Economy*, ed. Alan Harding, Alan Scott, Stephan Laske, and Christian Burtscher. (Burlington, VT: Ashgate, 2007), 95–118.

Bibliography

Adams, Carolyn. "The Meds and Eds in Urban Economic Development." *Journal of Urban Affairs* 25, no. 5 (2003): 571–588.

Ahles, Andrea. "Shooting, Recent Crimes Spark Outrage among Administrators." *Daily Pennsylvanian*, September 26, 1996. Available at http://www.dailypennsylvanian.com/node/8245.

Alessandri, Sue Westcott, Sung-Un Yang, and Dennis F. Kensey. "An Integrative Approach to University Visual Identity and Reputation." *Corporate Reputation Review* 9, no. 4 (2006): 258–270.

Allston Development Group (Cooper, Robertson & Partners, Gehry Partners, and Olin Partnership). *The Plan for Harvard in Allston (Draft): Executive Summary.* New York: Cooper, Robertson, 2007.

Anderson, Elijah. *Streetwise: Race, Class, and Change in an Urban Community.* Chicago: University of Chicago Press, 1990.

Austrian, Ziona, and Jill S. Norton. "An Overview of University Real Estate Investment Practices." In *The University as Urban Developer: Case Studies and Analysis*, edited by David C. Perry and Wim Wiewel, 193–221. Armonk, NY: M. E. Sharpe, 2005.

Bartelt, David W. "Renewing Center City Philadelphia: Whose City? Which Public Interests?" In *Unequal Partnerships: The Political Economy of Urban Redevelopment in Postwar America*, edited by Gregory D. Squires, 80–102. New Brunswick, NJ: Rutgers University Press, 1989.

Baruzzi, Cara. "Yale University Drives Downtown Retail Renewal." *New Haven Register*, October 30, 2005. Available at http://www.newhavenreg ister.com/articles/2005/10/30/import/15479564.txt.

Bates, Lisa K. *A Housing Submarket Approach to Neighborhood Planning: Theoretical Considerations and Empirical Justifications.* Ph.D. diss., University of North Carolina, Chapel Hill, 2006.

Baum, Howell S. "Fantasies and Realities in University–Community Partnerships." *Journal of Planning Education and Research* 20 (2000): 234–246.

———. "Smart Growth and School Reform: What If We Talked about Race and Took Community Seriously?" *Journal of the American Planning Association* 70, no. 1 (2004): 14–26.

Baye, Rachel. "Last Store Standing: The Restaurant Has Sparked Controversy among Administrators and Community Members over the Years." *Daily Pennsylvanian*, February 28, 2011. Available at http://thedp.com/index .php/article/2011/02/last_store_standing_the_past_and_present_of_ mcdonalds_at_40th_and_walnut.

Beauregard, Robert A. *Voices of Decline: The Postwar Fate of US Cities.* Cambridge, MA: Blackwell, 1993.

Bender, Thomas. "Scholarship, Local Life and the Necessity of Worldliness." In *The Urban University and its Identity*, edited by H. van der Wusten, 17–28. Dordrecht, Netherlands: Kluwer Academic Publishers, 1998.

———. *The University and the City: From Medieval Origins to Present.* New York: Oxford University Press, 1988.

Benson, Lee, and Ira Harkavy. "Saving the Soul of the University: What Is to Be Done?" In *The Virtual University: Knowledge, Markets and Management*, edited by Kevin Robins and Frank Webster, 169–209. Oxford: Oxford University Press, 2002.

Bissinger, H. G. *A Prayer for the City.* New York: Random House, 1997.

Bluestone, Barry, and Mary Huff Stevenson. *The Boston Renaissance: Race, Space, and Economic Change in an American Metropolis.* New York: Russell Sage Foundation, 2000.

Bok, Derek. *Universities and the Future of America.* Durham. NC: Duke University Press, 1990.

Calder, Allegra, Gabrial Grant, and Holly Hart Muson. "No Such Thing as Vacant Land: Northeastern University and Davenport Commons." In *The University as Urban Developer: Case Studies and Analysis*, edited by David C. Perry and Wim Wiewel, 253–267. Armonk, NY: M. E. Sharpe, 2005.

Campbell, Scott, and Susan S. Fainstein. "Introduction: The Structure and Debates of Planning Theory." In *Readings in Planning Theory*, 2nd. ed., edited by Scott Campbell and Susan S. Fainstein, 1–16. London: Blackwell, 2003.

Carweign, Vicky, Sandra Boyle, John Idstrom, and Mike Wark. "Capitalizing on Community: Turning Community Relations into the Biggest Asset of a New Campus." *Metropolitan Universities* 12, no. 2 (2001): 68–76.

Castells, Manuel. "The Informational City Is a Dual City: Can It Be Reversed?" In *High Technology and Low-Income Communities: Prospects for the Positive Use of Advanced Information Technology*, edited by Donald A. Schon, Bish Sanyal, and William Mitchell, 25–41. Cambridge: MIT Press, 1999.

CEOs for Cities and Initiative for a Competitive Inner City. *Leveraging Colleges and Universities for Urban Economic Revitalization: An Action Agenda*. Boston: ICIC, 2002. Available at http://www.ceosforcities.org/files/colleges_1.pdf.

Christopherson, Susan, and Jennifer Clark. *Remaking Regional Economies: Power, Labor and Firm Strategies in the Knowledge Economy*. New York: Routledge, 2009.

City of Philadelphia. "Neighborhood Transformation Initiative Progress Report, 2000–2003: Transforming Our Neighborhoods—Building Our Future." Report of the Philadelphia City Planning Commission, 2003.

City of Philadelphia Bureau of Revision and Taxes/Cartographic Modeling Laboratory. parcelBase Database. University of Pennsylvania, June 2006. Available at http://cml.upenn.edu/parcelbase/.

Clark, Burton R. *Creating Entrepreneurial Universities: Organizational Pathways of Transformation*. Paris: IAU Press, 1998.

Clay, Philip L. *Neighborhood Renewal: Middle-Class Resettlement and Incumbent Upgrading in American Neighborhoods*. Lexington, MA: Lexington Books, 1979.

Craig, David J. "Smart Growth: Columbia's Got a Long Range Plan to Advance Academics and Revitalize West Harlem." *Columbia Magazine*, June 2006, 8–15. Available at http://www.neighbors.columbia.edu/pages/manplanning/pdf-files/columbia_mag_june06.pdf.

Crooks, James. "The AUU and the Mission of the Urban University." *Urbanism Past and Present* 7, no. 2 (1982): 34–39.

Davidoff, Paul. "Advocacy and Pluralism in Planning." *Journal of the American Institute of Planners* 31 (November 1965): 331–338.

Delbanco, Andrew. "Scandals of Higher Education." *New York Review of Books*, March 29, 2007. Available at http://www.nybooks.com/articles/archives/2007/mar/29/scandals-of-higher-education/.

Dewan, Shaila. "Morehouse Searches for a Leader and a Way to Keep Making Gains." *New York Times*, March 28, 2007, B7.

Dobelle, Evan S. "Saviors of Our Cities: 2009 Survey of College and University Civic Partnerships." Fall 2009. Available at http://www.evandobelle.com/SOOC%20Survey%20Overview.pdf.

Dreier, Peter. "America's Urban Crisis: Symptoms, Causes and Solutions." In *Race, Poverty and American Cities*, edited by John Charles Boger with Judith Welch Wegner, 79–141. Chapel Hill: The University of North Carolina Press, 1996.

DuBois, W.E.B. *The Philadelphia Negro: A Social Study*. Philadelphia: University of Pennsylvania Press, 1996.

Duncan, O. D., and B. Duncan. *The Negro Population in Chicago*. Chicago: University of Chicago Press, 1957.

Edelman, Murray. "Political Language and Political Reality." *PS* 18, no. 1 (Winter 1985): 10–19.

Ellen, Ingrid, and Katherine M. O'Regan. "How Low Income Neighborhoods Change: Entry, Exit and Enhancement." *Regional Science and Urban Economics* 41, no. 2 (2011): 89–97.

Etienne, Harley. "University/Community Relations: Public Rhetoric and Private Interests." M.A. thesis, Temple University, 2001.

Evans, William N., and Emily Owens. "COPS and Crime." *Journal of Public Economics*, 91, no. 1–2 (February 2007): 181–201.

Fainstein, Susan S. *The City Builders: Property Development in New York and London, 1980–2000*. Lawrence: University Press of Kansas, 2001.

Fainstein, Susan S., and Norman Fainstein. Introduction to *Restructuring the City: The Political Economy of Urban Redevelopment*, rev. ed, edited by Susan Fainstein, Norman Fainstein, Richard Child Hill, Dennis Judd, and Michael P. Smith. New York: Longman, 1986.

Fainstein, Susan S., and Mia Gray. "Economic Development Strategies for the Inner City: The Need for Governmental Intervention." In *The Inner City: Urban Poverty and Economic Development in the Next Century*, edited by Thomas D. Boston and Catherine L. Ross, 29–38. New Brunswick, NJ: Transaction Publishers, 1997.

Faust, Drew Gilpin. "Allston Update Letter." *Harvard Gazette*, February 19, 2009. Available at http://news.harvard.edu/gazette/story/2009/02/allston-update-letter/.

Federal Bureau of Investigation. *Crime in the United States, 2005*. Washington: U.S. Department of Justice, Federal Bureau of Investigation, 2006.

Feller, Irwin. "S & T-Based Economic Development and the University: Virtuous and Vicious Cycles in the Contributions of Public Research Universities to State Economic Development Objectives." *Economic Development Quarterly* 18 no. 2 (2004): 138–150.

Felsenstein, Daniel. "The University in the Metropolitan Arena: Impacts and Public Policy Implications." *Urban Studies* 33, no. 9 (1996): 1565–1580.

Finder, Alan. "Headhunters at Harvard May Pick a Woman." *New York Times*, January 8, 2007. Available at http://www.nytimes.com/2007/01/08/education/08harvard.html.

Florida, Richard. *Cities and the Creative Class*. New York: Routledge, 2005.

———. "Place-Making after 9/11." In *Cities and the Creative Class*, 155–170. New York: Routledge, 2005.

Florida, Richard, and Wesley M. Cohen. "Engine or Infrastructure? The University Role in Economic Development." In *Industrializing Knowledge: University–Industry Linkages in Japan and the United States*, edited by Lewis M. Branscomb, Fumio Kodama, and Richard Florida, 589–610. Cambridge, MA: MIT Press, 1999.

Foderero, Lisa. "Critics Turn out at an Open House on N.Y.U. Expansion." *New York Times*, April 14, 2010. Available at http://www.nytimes.com/2010/04/15/nyregion/15nyu.html.

Fogarty, Michael S., and Amit K. Sinha. "Why Older Regions Can't Generalize from Route 128 and Silicon Valley: University–Industry Relationships and Regional Innovation Systems." In *Industrializing Knowledge: University–Industry Linkages in Japan and the United States*, edited by Lewis M. Branscomb, Fumio Kodama, and Richard Florida, 473–509. Cambridge, MA: MIT Press, 1999.

Forester, John F. "Conservative Epistemology, Reductive Ethics, Far Too Narrow Politics: Some Clarifications in Response to Yiftacheland Huxley." *International Journal of Urban and Regional Research* 24, no. 4 (2000): 914–16

———. *The Deliberative Practitioner: Encouraging Participatory Planning*. Cambridge, MA: MIT Press, 1999.

Freeland, Richard M. "Universities and Cities Need to Rethink Their Relationships." *Chronicle of Higher Education*, May 13, 2005, B20.

Freeman, Lance. "Displacement or Succession? Residential Mobility in Gentrifying Neighborhoods." *Urban Affairs Review* 40, no. 4 (2005): 463–491.

———. *There Goes the 'Hood: Views of Gentrification from the Ground Up*. Philadelphia: Temple University Press, 2006.

Frieden, Bernard, and Lynn Sagalyn. *Downtown, Inc.: How America Rebuilds Cities*. Cambridge, MA: MIT Press, 1989.

Gale, Dennis E. *Neighborhood Revitalization and the Postindustrial City*. Lexington, MA: Lexington Books, 1984.

Gibbons, Thomas J., Jr., and Nita Lelyveld. "A Halloween Homicide Jolts a Reeling Penn: Chemist Vladimir Sled Tried to Stop a Purse-Snatching and was Stabbed 5 Times." *Philadelphia Inquirer*, November 2, 1996, A1.

Gilderbloom John I., and R. L. Mullins, Jr. *Promise and Betrayal: Universities and the Battle for Sustainable Urban Neighborhoods*. Albany: State University of New York Press, 2005.

Godfrey, Brian J. "Tragedy and Transformation in New York City." *The Geographical Review* 92, no. 1 (January 2002): 127–139.

Goldin, Claudia, and Michael Katz. "The Shaping of Higher Education: The Formative Years in the United States." *Journal of Economic Perspectives* 13, no. 1 (1999): 37–62.

Goldstein, Harvey A., and Catherine S. Renault. "Contributions of Universities to Regional Economic Development: A Quasi-Experimental Approach." *Regional Studies* 38, no. 7 (2004): 733–746.

Greenwood, Davydd J. "Who Are the Real 'Problem Owners'? On the Social Embeddedness of Universities." In *Satanic Mills: Universities, The Knowledge Economy and Regional Development*, edited by Alan Harding, Alan Scott, Stephan Laske, and Christian Burtscher, 95–118. Burlington, VT: Ashgate, 2007.

Greenwood, Davydd J., and Morton Levin. "Reconstructing the Relationships between Universities and Society through Action Research." In *Handbook of Qualitative Research: Strategies for Qualitative Inquiry*, 2nd ed., edited by Norman K. Denzin and Yvonne S. Lincoln, 85–107. Thousand Oaks, CA: Sage Publications, 2003.

Grogan, Paul S., and Tony Proscio. *Comeback Cities: A Blueprint for Urban Neighborhood Revival*. Boulder, CO: Westview Press, 2000.

Gutmann, Amy. *Color Conscious: The Political Morality of Race*. Princeton, NJ: Princeton University Press, 1996.

———. *Why Deliberative Democracy*. Princeton, NJ: Princeton University Press, 2004.

Gutmann, Amy, with Kwame Appiah. *Democratic Education*. Princeton, NJ: Princeton University Press, 1987.

Gutmann, Amy, with Dennis Thompson. *Democracy and Disagreement*. Cambridge, MA: Belknap Press, 1996.

———. *Identity in Democracy*. Princeton, NJ: Princeton University Press, 2003.

Hackworth, Jason. *The Neoliberal City: Governance, Ideology, and Development in American Urbanism*. Ithaca, NY: Cornell University Press, 2007.

Harkavy, Ira. "The Demands of the Times and the American Research University." *Journal of Planning Literature* 1, no. 3 (1997): 333–336.

Harkavy, Ira, and John Puckett. "The Role of Mediating Structures in University and Community Revitalization: The University of Pennsylvania and West Philadelphia as a Case Study." *Journal of Research and Development in Education* 25, no. 1 (1991): 10–25.

———. "Universities and the Inner Cities." *Planning for Higher Education* 20, no. 4 (1992): 27–32.

Harkavy, Ira, and H. Zuckerman. "Eds and Meds: Cities' Hidden Assets." (Brookings Institution) *Survey Series*, August 1999, 1–6.

Harrison, Bennett. *Lean and Mean: The Changing Landscape of Corporate Power in the Age of Flexibility*. New York: Basic Books, 1994.

Harvey, David. "On Planning the Ideology of Planning." In *The Urbanization of Capital*, 165–184. Baltimore: Johns Hopkins University Press, 1985.

———. "The New Urbanism and the Communitarian Trap: On Social Problems and the False Hope of Design." *Harvard Design Magazine* 1 (Winter/Spring 1997): 1–3.

———. *The Urbanization of Capital: Studies in The History and Theory of Capitalist Urbanization*. Baltimore: Johns Hopkins University Press, 1985.

Heckathorn, Douglas S. "Respondent-Driven Sampling: A New Approach to the Study of Hidden Populations." *Social Problems* 44, no. 2 (1997): 174–199.

Hepp, Henry. *The Middle-Class City: Transforming Space and Time in Philadelphia, 1876–1926*. Philadelphia: University of Pennsylvania Press, 2003.

Hirsch, Arnold R. *Making the Second Ghetto: Race and Housing in Chicago, 1940–1960*. Chicago: University of Chicago Press, 1998.

Hirschman, Albert. *Exit, Voice, and Loyalty: Responses to Decline in Firms, Organizations, and States*. Cambridge, MA: Harvard University Press, 1970.

Hoover, E. M., and R. Vernon. *Anatomy of a Metropolis*. Cambridge, MA: Harvard University Press, 1959.

June, Audrey Williams. "As It Seeks More Room, Columbia Treads Carefully: A Planned $5-Billion Development in Neighboring Harlem Reawakens Old Animosities." *Chronicle of Higher Education*, October 1, 2004, A29.

Kasinitz, Philip. "Bringing the Neighborhood Back in the New Urban Ethnography." *Sociological Forum* 7, no. 2 (1992): 355–363.

Keating, W. Dennis. "Introduction: Neighborhoods in Urban America." In *Revitalizing Urban Neighborhoods*, edited by W. Dennis Keating, Norman Krumholz, and Philip Star, 1–6. Lawrence: University Press of Kansas, 1996.

Keller, S. *The Urban Neighborhood*. New York: Random House, 1968.

Kelnotic, Deborah. "Building a New Northeastern: The West Campus Residence Hall Opens an Era." *Northeastern University Magazine*, September 1999. Available at http://www.northeastern.edu/magazine/9909/westcamp.html.

Kerr, Clark. *The Uses of the University*, 5th ed. Cambridge, MA: Harvard University Press, 2001.

Klosterman, Richard E. "Arguments for and against Planning." *Town Planning Review* 56, no. 1 (1985): 5–20.

Klotsche, J. Martin. *The Urban University and the Future of Our Cities*. New York: Harper and Row, 1966.

Kodama, Fumio, and Lewis M. Branscomb. "University Research as an Engine for Growth: How Realistic Is the Vision?" In *Industrializing Knowledge: University–Industry Links in Japan and the United States*, edited by Lewis M. Branscomb, Fumio Kodama, and Richard Florida, 3–19. Cambridge, MA: MIT Press,1999.

Kromer, John, and Lucy Kerman. *West Philadelphia Initiatives: A Case Study in Urban Revitalization.* Philadelphia: University of Pennsylvania and Fels Institute of Government, 2005.

Lake, Robert W. "The Antiurban Angst of Urban Geography in the 1980s." *Urban Geography* 24, no. 4 (2003): 352–355.

Lauerman, John. "Harvard's Purcell to Advise on Expansion in Boston's Allston Neighborhood." *Bloomberg*, April 20, 2010. Available at http://www.bloomberg.com/news/2010-04-20/harvard-s-purcell-to-advise-on-expansion-in-boston-s-allston-neighborhood.html.

"Learning and Leading." *Pennsylvania Gazette* 103, no. 1 (September/October 2004): 30–37.

Lee, Trymaine. "Bracing for the Lion." *New York Times*, July 22, 2007, section 14, p. 1.

Lees, Loretta, Tom Slater, and Elvin K. Wyly. *Gentrification.* London: Routledge, 2008.

Lees, Lynn, Walter Licht, and Richard Shell. "Speaking Out: Neighborhood and Urban Agenda," *Penn Almanac* 43, no. 9 (1996). Available at http://www.upenn.edu/almanac/v43/n09/spouturb.html.

Levine, Donald N. "The Idea of the University, Take One: On the Genius of this Place." Paper presented at the Idea of the University Colloquium, University of Chicago, November 2000.

Loeterman, Dan. "Long-Term Community Residents Oppose USC Master Plan Details." Strategic Actions for a Just Economy, April 3, 2008. Available at http://www.saje.net/site/c.hkLQJcMUKrH/b.3998783/k.D068/Residents_Oppose_Master_Plan.htm.

Lowe, Herbert. "'Jump Street' Gets the Spotlight: Local Leaders Formally Announced the Development; They Expect Big Things for North Broad Street." *Philadelphia Inquirer*, July 7, 1998, B1.

Lynton, Ernest A., and Sandra E. Elman. *The New Priorities for the University.* San Francisco: Jossey-Bass Publishers, 1987.

Marcuse, Peter, and Cuz Potter. "Columbia University's Heights: An Ivory Tower and Its Communities." In *The University as Urban Developer: Case Studies and Analysis*, edited by David C. Perry and Wim Wiewel, 45–64. Armonk, NY: M. E. Sharpe, 2005.

"Market Value Analysis: Philadelphia." Reinvestment Fund, 2006. Available at http://www.trfund.com/planning/market-phila.html.

"A Marriage Meant to Be: Amy Gutmann Inaugurated as Penn's Eighth President." *Pennsylvania Gazette* 103, no. 2 (2004). 30–41.

Marris, Peter. *Loss and Change.* London: Routledge, 1986.

Martindale, Scott. "Defining Downtown: USC Boundaries Expanding within Limits." *Daily Trojan*, November 14, 2001, 2–8.

Massey, Douglas S., and Nancy A. Denton. *American Apartheid: Segregation and the Making of the Underclass*. Cambridge, MA: Harvard University Press, 1993.

Maurasse, David J. *Beyond the Campus: How Colleges and Universities Form Partnerships with Their Communities*. New York: Routledge, 2001.

McClelland, Charles E. "'To Live for Science': Ideals and Realities at the University of Berlin." In *The University and the City*, edited by Thomas Bender, 181–197. Oxford: Oxford University Press, 1988.

McGovern, Stephen J. "Philadelphia's Neighborhood Transformation Initiative: A Case Study of Mayoral Leadership, Bold Planning, and Conflict." *Housing Policy Debate* 17, no. 3 (2006): 529–570.

McKenzie, Roderick D. "The Ecological Approach to the Study of Human Community." In *The City*, ed. Robert Park and Ernest Burgess, 287–301. Chicago: University of Chicago Press, 1925.

Meyers, Allen. *The Jewish Community of West Philadelphia*. Mt. Pleasant, SC: Arcadia Publishing, 2001.

Muller, Thomas. *Immigrants and the American City*. New York: New York University Press, 1993.

National Commission on Excellence in Education. *A Nation at Risk: The Imperative for Educational Reform*. Washington, DC: Government Printing Office, 1983.

Nelson, Daniel. *Frederick W. Taylor and the Rise of Scientific Management*. Madison: University of Wisconsin Press, 1980.

Newfield, Christopher, *Ivy and Industry: Business and the Making of the American University, 1880–1980*. Durham, NC: Duke University Press, 2003.

Newman, John Henry. *The Idea of a University*. Edited by Frank M. Turner. New Haven, CT: Yale University Press, 1996.

Newman, Katherine S. *No Shame in My Game: The Working Poor in the Inner City*. New York: Alfred A. Knopf and the Russell Sage Foundation, 1999.

Nussbaum, Paul. "SEPTA Celebrates End of Market Street El Work." *Philadelphia Inquirer*, September 12, 2009, B2.

O'Mara, Margaret Pugh. *Cities of Knowledge: Cold War Science and the Search for the Next Silicon Valley*. Princeton, NJ: Princeton University Press, 2005.

Palen, J. John, and Bruce London, eds. *Gentrification, Displacement and Neighborhood Revitalization*. Albany: State University of New York Press, 1984.

Park, Robert A. *Human Communities*. Glencoe, IL: Free Press, 1952.

Park, Robert E., with Ernest W. Burgess, Roderick McKenzie, and Louis Wirth. *The City*. Chicago: University of Chicago Press, 1925.

Pattillo-McCoy, Mary. "The Limits of Out-Migration for the Black Middle Class." *Journal of Urban Affairs* 22, no. 3 (Fall 2000): 225–241.

Peattie, Lisa R. "Reflections in Advocacy Planning." *Journal of the American Institute of Planners* 34, no. 2 (1968): 80–87.

Prendergast, John. "Learning and Leading," *Pennsylvania Gazette* 103, no. 1 (September–October 2004): 30–37.

Perry, David C., and Wim Wiewel. "From Campus to City: The University as Developer." In *The University as Urban Developer: Case Studies and Analysis*, edited by David C. Perry and Wim Wiewel, 3–21. Armonk, NY: M. E. Sharpe, 2005.

———. *The University as Urban Developer.* Armonk, NY: M. E. Sharpe, 2005.

Quigley, John M., and Steven Raphael. "Is Housing Unaffordable? Why Isn't It More Affordable?" *Journal of Economic Perspectives* 18, no. 1 (2004): 191–214.

Quillian, Lincoln, and Devah Pager. "Black Neighbors, Higher Crime? The Role of Racial Stereotypes in Evaluations of Neighborhood Crime." *American Journal of Sociology* 107, no. 3 (2001): 717–763.

Richards, William. "Architecture's Communards at Columbia." Paper presented at the Annual Meetings of the Association of American Geographers, Washington, DC, April 2010.

Riposa, Gerry. "From Enterprise Zones to Empowerment Zones." *American Behavioral Scientist* 39, no. 5 (1996): 536–551.

Rodin, Judith. "The Inaugural Address." *(University of Pennsylvania) Almanac* 41, no. 9 (October 25, 1994): S-4–S-7. Available at http://www.upenn.edu/almanac/v41pdf/n09/102594-insert.pdf.

———. "The 21st Century Urban University: New Roles for Practice and Research." *Journal of the American Planning Association* 71, no. 3 (2005): 237–249.

———. *The University and Urban Revival: Out of the Ivory Tower and into the Streets.* Philadelphia: University of Pennsylvania Press, 2007.

"The Rodin Years." *Pennsylvania Gazette* 105, no. 4 (May–June 2007): 33–41.

Rubin, Herbert. "Shoot Anything That Flies, Claim Anything That Falls: Conversations with Economic Development Practitioners." *Economic Development Quarterly* 2, no. 3 (1988): 236–251.

Rubin, Victor. "The Roles of Universities in Community-Building Initiatives." *Journal of Planning Education and Research* 17, no. 4 (1998): 302–311.

Saffron, Inga. "Welcome Back, Girard Avenue: A Street Reborn—Girard Avenue Revival." *Philadelphia Inquirer*, January 9, 2004, E1.

Sagalyn, Lynne B. *Times Square Roulette: Remaking the City Icon.* Cambridge, MA: MIT Press, 2000.

Sanjek, Roger. "Network Organization and Its Uses in Urban Ethnography." *Human Organization* 37, no. 3 (1978): 257–268.

Saxenian, AnnaLee. *Regional Advantage: Culture and Competition in Silicon Valley and Route 128.* Cambridge, MA: Harvard University Press, 1994.

Schwirian, Kent P. "Models of Neighborhood Change." *Annual Review of Sociology* 9 (1983): 83–102.

Seyffert, M. Gordon. "The University as Urban Neighbor." In *Universities in the Urban Crisis,* edited by T. P. Murphy, 137–159. New York: Dunellen Publishing, 1975.

Simmons, Patrick A., and Robert E. Lang. *The Urban Turnaround: A Decade-by-Decade Report Card on Postwar Population Change in Older Industrial Cities.* Washington, DC: The Fannie Mae Foundation, 2001.

Slater, Tom. "The Eviction of Critical Perspectives from Gentrification Research." *International Journal of Urban and Regional Research* 30, no. 4 (2006): 737–757.

Slaughter, Sheila, and Larry L. Leslie. *Academic Capitalism: Politics, Policies and the Entrepreneurial University.* Baltimore: Johns Hopkins University Press, 1997.

Smith, Neil. *The New Urban Frontier: Gentrification and the Revanchist City.* London: Routledge, 1996.

———. *Uneven Development: Nature, Capital, and the Production of Space.* Athens: University of Georgia Press, 2008.

Stack, Carol B. *All Our Kin: Strategies for Survival in a Black Community.* New York: Harper and Row, 1974.

Stukel, J. J. "The Urban University Attacks Real Urban Issues." *Government Finance Review* 10, no. 5 (1994): 19–21.

Sugrue, Thomas. *The Origins of the Urban Crisis: Race and Inequality in Postwar Detroit.* Princeton, NJ: Princeton University Press, 2005.

———. "Revisiting the Second Ghetto." *Journal of Urban History* 29 (2003): 281.

Talen, Emily. "The Problem with Community." *Journal of Planning Literature* 15 (2000): 171–183.

Taub, Richard, with D. Garth Taylor and Jan D. Dunham. *Paths of Neighborhood Change: Race and Crime in Urban America.* Chicago: University of Chicago Press, 1984.

Teaford, Jon C. *The Rough Road to Renaissance: Urban Revitalization in America, 1940–1985.* Baltimore: Johns Hopkins University Press, 1990.

Teitz, Michael B., and Karen Chapple. "The Causes of Inner-City Poverty: Eight Hypotheses in Search of Reality. *Cityscape: A Journal of Policy Development and Research* 3, no. 3 (1998): 33–70.

Terino, John George, Jr. "In the Shadow of Spreading Ivy: Science, Culture and the Cold War at the University of Pennsylvania, 1950–1970." Ph.D. diss., University of Pennsylvania, 2001.

Thomas, George E. *The Campus Guide: University of Pennsylvania.* New York: Princeton Architectural Press, 2002.

Thomas, George E., and David Brownlee. *Building America's First University: An Historical and Architectural Guide to the University of Pennsylvania.* Philadelphia: University of Pennsylvania Press, 2000.

Thomas, June Manning. "Rebuilding Inner Cities: Basic Principles." In *The Inner City: Urban Poverty and Economic Development in the Next Century,* edited by Thomas Boston and Catherine Ross, 67–74. New Brunswick, NJ: Transaction Publishers, 1999.

———. *Redevelopment and Race.* Baltimore: Johns Hopkins University Press, 1997.

Thomas, Wendy. "Store's Closure a Blow to USC Neighborhood." *Los Angeles Times,* September 30, 2005. Available at http://articles.latimes.com/2005/sep/30/local/me-market30.

Travers, Eva. "Philadelphia School Reform: Historical Roots and Reflections on the 2002–2003 School Year under State Takeover." *Penn GSE Perspectives on Urban Education* 2, no. 2 (Fall 2003). Available at http://www.urbanedjournal.org/archive/Issue4/commentaries/comment0007.html.

Tyler, Jean B., and Martin Maberman. "Education–Community Partnerships: Who Uses Whom and for What Purposes?" *Metropolitan Universities* 13, no. 4 (2002): 88–100.

University City District. *University City Report Card, 2006.* Philadelphia: University City District, 2007, 17.

———. *University City Report Card 2007.* Philadelphia: University City District, 2007.

University of Pennsylvania. "Appendix III: Digest of Valley Forge Plan." Board of trustees meeting minutes, May 22, 1936. Available at http://www.archives.upenn.edu/primdocs/uplan/valforgemay1936.pdf.

———. *Penn Economic Impact Report, FY 2010.* Available at http://www.evp.upenn.edu/docs/PennEconomicImpact_SlideShow.pdf.

———. "The Radian: Project Overview." Penn Connects. Available at http://www.pennconnects.upenn.edu/find_a_project/completed/completed_2008/the_radian_overview.php.

———. "University History: Penn Campuses before 1900," Penn University Archives and Records Center. Available at http://www.archives.upenn.edu/histy/features/campuses/tour.html.

University of Southern California. "University Park Campus Master Planning." Available at http://www.usc.edu/community/upcmasterplan/.

———. "USC Master Plan 2030—Fact Sheet," May 27, 2008. Available at http://www.nandc.org/docs/land_use/USCMstrPlan-FinalMtgDocs.pdf.

U.S. Department of Housing and Urban Development. *Building Communities Together.* Washington, DC: Government Printing Office, 1994.

————.*Urban Empowerment Zones and Enterprise Communities.* HUD-1551-CPD. Washington, DC: Government Printing Office, 1995.

Van der Wusten, Herman, ed. *The Urban University and Its Identity.* Dordrecht, Netherlands: Kluwer Academic Publishers, 1998.

Varady, David P., and Jeffrey A. Raffel. *Selling Cities: Attracting Homebuyers through Schools and Housing Programs.* Albany, NY: State University of New York Press, 1995.

VerMeulen, Michael. "The University as Landlord." *Institutional Investor* 14, no. 5 (1980): 119–122.

Vest, Charles M. "Higher Education: A Key Economic Asset." Paper presented to the Greater Boston Chamber of Commerce, Boston, January 22, 1996.

————. *Pursuing the Endless Frontier: Essays on MIT and the Role of Research Universities.* Cambridge, MA: MIT Press, 2005.

Wacquant, Loïc J. D., and William Julius Wilson. "The Cost of Racial and Class Exclusion in the Inner City." *Annals of the American Academy of Political and Social Science* 501 (January 1989): 8–25.

Ward, Patrick. "Retail Monopoly Bad for Shoppers, Profits." *Yale Daily News*, March 27, 2007. Available at http://www.yaledailynews.com/news/2007/mar/27/retail-monopoly-bad-for-shoppers-profits.

Weber, Rachel. "Extracting Value from the City: Neoliberalism and Urban Development." *Antipode* 34, no. 3 (2002): 519–540.

Wee, Gillian. "Harvard to Raise 'Several Hundred Million' from Property Sales." *Bloomberg*, February 17, 2010. Available at http://www.bloomberg.com/apps/news?pid=washingtonstory&sid=aZWJS44lDy4M.

Whyte, William Foote. *Street Corner Society: the Social Structure of an Italian Slum.* Chicago: University of Chicago Press, 1943.

Williams, Brett. *Upscaling Downtown: Stalled Gentrification in Washington, D.C.* Ithaca, NY: Cornell University Press.

Willis, Paul. *Learning to Labor: How Working Class Kids Get Working Class Jobs.* New York: Columbia University Press, 1982.

Wilson, David. *Cities and Race: America's New Black Ghetto.* London: Routledge, 2007.

Wilson, James Q. "Planning and Politics: Citizen Participation in Urban Renewal." In *Urban Renewal: The Record and the Controversy*, edited by James Q. Wilson, 407–421. Cambridge, MA: MIT Press, 1966.

Wilson, William Julius. *The Truly Disadvantaged: The Inner City, the Underclass and Public Policy.* Chicago: University of Chicago Press, 1987.

————. *When Work Disappears: The World of the New Urban Poor.* New York: Vantage Books, 1996.

Wilson, William Julius, and Richard P. Taub. *There Goes the Neighborhood: Racial, Ethnic and Class Tensions in Four Chicago Neighborhoods and Their Meaning for America.* New York: Alfred A. Knopf, 2006.

Winter, Gene. "Jacuzzi U.? A Battle of Perks to Lure Students." *New York Times*, October 5, 2003, 1. Available at http://www.nytimes.com/2003/10/05/us/jacuzzi-u-a-battle-of-perks-to-lure-students.html?pagewanted=all&src=pm.

Index

Harley Etienne is an Assistant Professor of Urban and Regional Planning in the Taubman College of Architecture and Urban Planning at the University of Michigan.